THIS SEETHING OCEAN, THAT DAMNED EAGLE

THIS SEETHING OCEAN, THAT DAMNED EAGLE

Caleb Powell

Reflected Images Publishers

Library of Congress Card Number
93-087018

ISBN 1-878815-04-0

Reflected Images Publishers
P.O.Box 314
Medford, Oregon 97501

THIS SEETHING OCEAN, THAT DAMNED EAGLE

Part I

...the eyes that fix you in a formulated phrase
and when I am formulated, sprawling on a pin
when I am pinned and wriggling on the wall
then how shall I begin
to spit out all the butt-ends of my days and ways

—T. S. Eliot

I have been troubled by life in my youth, as have many others. I spent a great portion of time searching for purpose, considering myself on a self-imposed quest for meaning. Now, in my next stage of life, I look at the absurdity of my attempts to place importance on this or that. Doubtless I am who I am because of my experiences, yet I missed the point. If I had only known that trying to find meaning is like looking for God in a bowl of cereal.

I was raised in a town in northwestern Washington. The sea is in the town, and the moss covering the shingles of the hundred-year-old buildings on Front Street, and the seagull-and-fish-stained dock. Elderly people wander in and out of shops, restaurants, and taverns. They complain about rain and the wind that blows in from the Pacific, and praise summer and leisure. The sea is in their routine, and in them. People move from the city to raise a family or retire, and the small-town life slowly addicts them.

My parents met at college. My father studied architecture, my mother, music. They married after college and went overseas as my father was in the military. On their return, my father became a civilian and found a job in Seattle. They lived in the city for five years, all the time waiting for a child to be born as they could not have their own. When I was born they adopted me and gave me the name of Paul Matthew Taylor. My father then took a job away from the city and we became residents of this town.

As I grew up, I attended school and played with other children. I took vacations with my parents and went trick-or-treating at Halloween and on Christmas Eve I would stay up past midnight. Every Sunday I went to church and Sunday school. I remember my Sunday school teacher beaming as she looked forward to heaven, "...if you fall in heaven an angel shall catch you, for there can be no pain...". My childhood must have been wonderful.

At the north end of town was a dock and nestled in pine, cedar and madrona trees a quarter mile away from the dock and at the top of a cliff was our house; a wooden A-frame. The land slowly went inward along the coast and from the dock to our house, so we could not see the town. Our view consisted of trees, rocky beach, and the sea. This more than compensated for not having a television set. The house was full of artifacts for me to examine, discover, and amuse myself with: marble statues, miniature wooden dragons, paintings and scrolls from Asia, slabs of marble and jade, Chinese screens and many books. I looked at every book I could find; with diverse topics ranging from the poisonous and non-poisonous snakes of Taiwan to an anthology of cartoons. There were pages of poetry, endless novels, philosophy, history; knowledge both common and eclectic. I would look over them all, even the ones filled with music, for I liked reading over the titles of songs and trying to guess what the song sounded like by looking at written notes. Sometimes I'd ask my mother to play a request, and when she did it sounded nothing like I expected. When she finished she would look at me and smile, usually saying nothing. My mother, slim and small, her hair beginning to turn gray and silver, rarely said anything.

The living room walls were lined with bookcases, paintings, and odds and ends my parents had picked up through life. A brown and orange rug inlaid with dragons covered the floor of the room, surrounded by chairs and couches. A piano was in a corner, facing the ocean. My parents' room, the kitchen and dining room, a bathroom, and my father's study, were also downstairs. My room, which overlooked the sea, and a room for storage, were upstairs. There was plenty of space for a family of three.

The lawns encircling our house weren't really lawns, but

patches of grass, bare earth, and a few islands of flowers and bark, with a stone path winding in and between trees and shrubbery. Our backyard had more grass than the front, and there was a clearing obstructed by one madrona tree that opened to the sky and sea. I would stand by that madrona tree and look down the bluff seeing whitecaps fade as they washed ashore.

I remember when I was at elementary school my classmates would talk about the great TV shows they watched: those "Bionic People," "Battlestar Galactica," "The Incredible Hulk" and Saturday morning cartoons. I was curious about these shows I never saw and brought this up to my father. He'd say, "Paul, with all the things you can do, you don't need television. While your school pals are filling their minds with garbage and junk you'll be feeding your mind."

Sometimes I would complain about boredom but my father would tell me, "If you want to earn the money for your own television set, you are free to do so, but I won't spend a penny on one." I only sort of wanted a television, and for the most part I did fine without one. Now I am thankful that I had to find things to do.

My parents spent their time reading or partaking in other leisurely activities. My father had a lathe in the garage and would make wooden bowls in his spare time. My mother played the piano, cooked and kept house. We'd all help doing chores and yard work. Time passed with relative ease in our satisfied household.

My parents were Christian and this influence played upon me. We prayed at mealtime, went to church regularly, celebrated Easter and Christmas; if my father stubbed his toe he might mutter a "Dammit to hell"' and then he'd say, "Forgive me, Lord." My parents were not overzealous. They were religious but never preached or pushed it on me or anyone.

And they seemed to agree upon every thing. I cannot remember any argument or exchange of words filled with animosity or even petty annoyance between them. If they did argue it was not in my presence. When they disagreed they would discuss the matter civilly. If my father forbade me to climb on the bluff at night I would look at my mother and she'd nod, "Your father's right."

By the time I reached high school, however, I wasn't forbidden much. I had my parents trust. I stayed out late and came and went as I pleased but I never caused problems. I wasn't social, had no bad crowd to mix with, and by my sophomore year I kept to myself. As well, churchgoing tapered off. I found church dull and felt, because I believed in God, there was no need to go. I was at an age that my parents didn't see any necessity in my continuing, although they still went every once in a while.

At this point I began reading philosophy. I was introduced to utilitarianism, existentialism, empiricism, determinism, and contradiction. I fed upon philosophy. Life, death, God, existence, immortality; all of a sudden they had significance for my naive perception. It was a thrill to read a first person journey into a great mind; asking and wondering why we were here, discarding the trivial routines of everyday life for a higher knowledge. I relished cynical accounts of the ignorance of humanity. How true they seemed! Men were and are fools! So far I was from realizing my own irrelevance. I took pleasure in the appearance of separation, that I was different, taking my first peek at knowledge infinite, while others fervently prepared for Homecoming week.

Undoubtedly my growth was gradual, but it seems as if for a period of time I was simply rather fascinated with philosophy. I spent time reading or contemplating in isolation perched on the hard, burnt red branches of madrona trees, peeling off the skin or bark until sunset. Sometimes I would walk the quarter mile to town and stand on the dock, the breeze parting my short dark hair every which way. I always wore jeans and if it was cold I wore my dark green army jacket. I was vain, but I wished to appear intelligent and wise. The high school fashion carnival wasn't for me. If I were to be in a crowd, best that I wasn't noticed. The dock was solitary at night, going a hundred yards out into the ocean, and at its end was a store with a deli that sold sandwiches, fishing tackle and bait, as well as souvenirs. At a right angle a ramp went down to a floating dock where boats could tie up for a spell. I liked going there at night, when the store was closed and the boats were asleep and I would pass time with the moon and its shimmering reflection on the black opaque ocean. I went through a narcissistic build up, with an infantile acknowledgement that death was at the end and we either existed by cruel chance or by a splendid cohesion, and that I was one of the few that realized this. At first the answer mattered little, but gradually thoughts accumulated, people seemed as sensible as driftwood, only those who wished to discover purpose ... at first the answer mattered little, but slowly my concern grew, until one evening, I was seventeen and in the fall of my senior year, I realized nothing made sense, and this bothered me when before it only interested me. God ceased to be a fascinating concept but an enigma whose solution was essential. I reflected; nothing made sense, my parents, teachers, and peers all appeared to lead useless lives. Seasons changed, dreams hovered over people's heads and I thought they were all deceiving themselves. From the pictures I had seen in *National Geographic* I knew there was beauty on every continent, to see everything would take a lifetime, but if one cannot be satisfied with beauty then what is there? Other kids my age were experiencing their first kiss. I knew I was going to die.

I stood on the dock, thinking about death; numb and dumb, I thought about death. What I considered reality struck me: If life wasn't enjoyable then death wouldn't be a problem, it would almost be welcome; if death wasn't a problem life might be enjoyable. The moon lay in silver shivers on the ocean, almost touching my feet at the edge of the dock. I could jump in and swim deep into the water and I'd drown and I'd be dead. But I didn't. I turned away and stepped on the sparkling, frosted timbers of the dock and headed for home. Upon entering my father said, "Hello Paul, you're looking cheerful, as usual."

"Uh huh," I walked by,

"Paul," I stopped and looked at my father, who continued, "Are you happy?"

"Happy?"

"Yeah, happy. Do you care about anything?"

And so I answered, "Death."

"Death? What concerns you about death?"

"Well, death doesn't matter-"

"So you care about something that doesn't matter?" His eyebrows were lowered. My father resemebled me closely enough to be mistaken for my actual father. He was almost fifty, but looked younger. He still had some black hair mixed in with gray, and he was almost as tall as me and of the same build, slender and of average height. Although I was a teen he was slightly leaner than I.

"No, I think death's important."

His brow wrinkled more, "So, then, what do you mean?"

"You die, I die, so what? Death doesn't matter. Think of all the people who are now dead. What do they matter?"

"They matter to us."

"It's no consolation."

My father tapped his finger on the table and grimaced. He rarely got excited, was amiable about everything; an aura of contentment usually surrounded him. "So you don't care if you die?"

I answered, "No, I'd be dead," there was a long pause and I explained, "I guess I'd be in heaven, right? It'd almost be better if you or I died, don't you think?"

"Then why live?"

"Exactly, what's the point? You believe in God, you go to heaven. That makes your life bliss. But what about the screwed up kid who doesn't know any better, winds up in jail early, and in hell for eternity? Why aren't we just born in heaven or hell, why live in this purgatory? As for me, I don't know, flip a coin, who cares?"

"There's more to heaven and hell than that."

"There better be."

My father let out a deep breath, "So, if your mother or I died, you wouldn't care? You wouldn't be sad at all?"

"Nope. If I died you'd go on living, and if you died I guess I'd have to continue. As the world turns my life would be affected. But for better or worse, I don't know."

I felt my father's gaze as I left the room.

And I went upstairs to my room and looked at the moon. It was full and high in the sky, and in the quiet night I yearned for a spider's web to fill the corner of my window so I could watch a spider dance in the moonlight. I remember my father's eyes, blue-gray, momentarily stunned, as if they suddenly and slightly got bigger and then returned to normal size as his calm expression returned. I felt awful. There I was fearing death, mine, and now my father's. I loved my father, I realized as sentiment welled inside, and the spider that wasn't there twisted and danced while I lay there unable to weep.

As I drifted into a semi-conscious state I saw my myself falling, my plummet was stopped abruptly by a spike, impaling me like an hors' d'oeuvre on a toothpick. In bed this image of falling was easy to imagine. This was what I deserved, and from that moment I would find myself stuck upon the black silhouette of the spike again and again.

The spike changed me, for it told me I was alone; I was disassociated from my parents and peers. There I was, stuck on a spike. Other people, when they felt awkward or embarrassed might imagine a bucket of water poured over themselves or a pie in their face, but for me it was the spike. I needed a change.

When Dennis, a fellow senior, invited me to a party I accepted. I knew more about Dennis than I did about most of my schoolmates, as I had two classes with him and sat next to him in one of them. Dennis had cereal box good looks; curly, sandy blonde hair and freckles. He talked about girls and parties which he occasionally invited me to but I had never accepted. I thought alcohol probably didn't lead to virtue, but might at least offer experience and a different point of view, from which knowledge might derive.

Dennis picked me up in his red Dodge Dart, which he affectionately called his 'partymobile'. He talked freely, and I felt comfortable as he spoke, "You got a really cool pad, man. I'd do anything to live where you do."

I laughed aloud, and Dennis asked, "So, what made you accept my offer this time?"

"I needed a change."

"From what?" Dennis glanced sideways at me as he drove, "You're the one guy I've never figured. You're normal, I think, at least you're not a nerd, but you never do anything with anyone. I've heard your name mentioned by girls, they think you're shy, girls like shy guys." He grinned at me.

"I guess I keep to myself," I told Dennis, who filled me in on the party. We were going to Lisa's house; her parents were away. Lisa was a senior whom I knew little about. We arrived at a two story house in a neighborhood of similar houses. The two of us went inside, and Dennis soon found someone else to talk to, leaving me in the midst of familiar faces. I didn't know anyone, however, and I felt as uncomfortable as bare feet on ice. There was a wall near a window that looked like it could be a perfect space for me to fill, and I stood there and observed. I looked at the cluster of people in the living room around a coffee table playing beer games. I was not going to get drunk the first time there.

As I stood glued to the wall, a fellow approached me and said, "How's it going, buddy? I'm Frank," Frank offered me his claw to shake, which I did, and Frank went on, "This is great, I'm fucked up, are you?"

I looked at Frank, "Yup."

"Wachoo been drinking?"

"Nothing."

Frank tried to stand still, "You on drugs?"

"Nope."

Frank frowned, and looked for someone else to breathe upon. Everyone was drinking, and they appeared to be having a good time, listening to rock music. I didn't mind rock music, I just never listened to it, but this music was too loud. All this seemed vapid and I began to despise it. Some idiots were smoking cigarettes, I wanted to leave, I wandered outside and found a hidden tree to stand underneath, and I waited for Dennis to come out. My wait was long, probably over an hour and perhaps two, and when he came out I met him at the car. He said he'd looked all over for me, and asked me where I'd gone. I told him I'd taken a walk.

Dennis was able to drive home because he had spent more time with Lisa than he did drinking. He asked me, "You have a good time?"

"Not really," I replied," I've never been drunk."

"You're shittin' me!" I couldn't tell whether he was sarcastic or not.

"I'd like to get drunk, but somewhere else, alone."

Dennis was silent.

I asked him, "Could you help me?"

He shrugged, "Sure, in a way it's my duty," he laughed at his comment, I'll tell you what I'm gonna do. I've got about half a fifth of this dude Jack stashed in my room. It's yours."

"Free?"

"Why not? I mean, you've never been drunk. The first one's on me."

"Thanks."

"Besides, I'm in a good mood. I got laid."

"What?"

"I screwed Lisa."

I couldn't imagine, and I murmured, "Uh huh."

We drove to his home, and he went inside. He came back with the fifth of whiskey. It was actually only a third full, and I wondered if it would be enough. Dennis assured me it would fuck me up. He took me home and I thanked him again. I went to my room, stuck the bottle in an old model airplane box, and fell asleep.

The next evening I went along a hiking trail that went from the dock, past our house, and for miles north at the top of the bluff. I came to a spot a half mile away from our house, with sleeping bag, a tea cup, the Jack Daniels, and a box of Ritz crackers. I poured the cup a quarter full and stared at the whiskey. Wishing I had brought a clear glass, I smelled the alcohol. The pungent odor went up my nose like salt water. I built my nerve and gulped it. I repeated this, I'm not sure how many times.

When I finished I was revolving counter-clockwise in a clockwise world. The sun was toasting the day with a scarlet, orange, pink and red wine, and I felt alive. The sky passed through shades of blue, and as I saw the first star I looked at my box of crackers. On the box it said, 'Everything tastes better on a Ritz.' Pulling out a handful I placed one on top of the other. I thought this was hilarious. I ate crackers, but the alcohol was the dominant taste in my throat.

I considered Dennis. His priority was sex. I was a virgin, even my lips were virgin, and the thought of holding a girl for an extended period of time seemed bliss aplenty. The idea of sex was foreign, and I wasn't sure how to feel about Dennis' attitude toward sex, but I wondered if, for him, having sex was more important than the girl. It was true, I acted shy around girls, and even around guys I kept to myself, but with guys I didn't feel uncomfortable.

The stars and the night took me, and I began to think about my present state. For intellectual stimulation? An answer to the riddle of life and death and existence? I took a piss, thinking about God and heaven and hell. Jesus, I was drunk! I fell down on my sleeping bag and saw dark branches in the night light. Creation? God or no God? Evolution? God and Satan and piss running down the edge of the bluff and onto the corner of my sleeping bag.

This was dreadfully funny, and I laughed hard instead of bothering to move the sleeping bag. I wondered what it might be like to be drunk in a social setting. For this short while I enjoyed myself. I realized I had no friends. This seemed neither good nor bad. My parents stayed out of my life, giving me freedom, asking me how I was doing and what I did, but never what I thought. They spent a lot of time with one another, occasionally eating out or taking a trip somewhere over the weekend. My father was satisfied in working and coming home. My mother played the piano, cooked, kept house, but what she did all day I was unsure. She was so silent I thought she had nothing to say. She was slight and short, with long, light brown hair and streaks of gray, which was the only evidence of her age. She was a year younger than my father.

I began to feel sick, and the nausea made me so uncomfortable that I stood and retched over the bluff. I took no notice of the view. I gathered my belongings and went home, feeling a little better after throwing up. On returning I washed the rancid corner of my sleeping bag at an outside faucet. My pant leg got wet in the process. I lay the bag in my room to dry, and went to bed. As I shifted into sleep I thought about my father. I assured myself he knew I loved him. This reasoning satisfied me for the time being.

Upon waking I felt like my head was between concrete and

an anvil. I looked out the window, but it was painted light blue and white, and I closed my eyes and stayed in bed until numb became pain. I took three aspirin and went downstairs to eat breakfast.

That week at school Dennis asked me if I had drunk the whiskey. I said I had.

Dennis asked, "Were you fucked up?"

"How could I not be?"

"You like it?"

I rolled my lips to the side and mused, "Hmmmm, yes and no. It was different."

"Well, if you want to get drunk sometime, you know who to look for."

"I'll keep that in mind," I said.

I didn't think I'd ever take Dennis up on his offer. To me, drinking more than once meant a step toward alcoholism. Besides, I already felt I knew what it was like to be drunk.

That afternoon, I walked to a madrona tree a little ways from our house. It was a perfect place to perch. The tree, knotted and gnarled, stood in the ground as the cliff sloped downwards. Off in the distance, above the ocean and a few hundred yards out from the cliff against a cloudy sky flew the eagle. The eagle had its nest in a pine tree a distance away, and it frequently circled the ocean. I wished I could trade places with it.

The eagle. Destiny. Somehow I was convinced I was destined to find out the purpose of my life, and in the process discover the purpose of life in general. I didn't know this is a personal, not universal, fulfillment. Since I had a strong desire and interest in discovering universal meaning I assumed there was a likelihood in achieving my goal. I never considered the fact that the greatest minds, those of philosophers, prophets, writers, scientists, and artists; as well as the minds of the not-so-great; throughout the ages, had been unsuccessful in this pursuit. Like many young do-gooders, it was not so much a concern of mine that humanity be helped as much as that I help humanity. I didn't know what I'd do after high school, my grades were good, but I wasn't sure if education could help me in my search. I was beginning to think that if I could discover the meaning of life then

I could tell the world, and world peace would be possible as the word spread. There I was, unable to communicate with my parents, yet I was able to seriously entertain this plan to help mankind. The wind blew through me, around me, and into me. As dusk creeped up the coast I stroked the smooth madrona. The eagle disappeared and I had discovered my purpose: To find purpose.

As darkness fell I walked home through the trees. When I was younger I had intentionally found a spooky place in the woods at night, and I sat there until my fear of the dark left. Now night meant peace. There is soothing calm in a black and blue world.

School droned by. Occasionally I would see someone I recognized from the party. I hadn't thought I'd remember anyone, but more than once I saw someone stare at me and I suspected he or she had seen me pressed against the wall at Lisa's house. I became even more withdrawn. Wrapping myself up in pride and ego at one of my most confused periods in my life, I was convinced I was aimed in the right direction.

Although night is enjoyable the short days of winter add to the dismal effect of poor weather. It snowed on the first day of Christmas break. No matter how bitter the bite of ice and snow, or how wicked the cold was, I was glad to see snow. The buildings, trees, rocks, the dock, were covered with a white layer.

Wrapped in clothes and carrying a thermos of hot chocolate or soup I contemplated the thoughts that led to the discovery of more thoughts. My first step would be to solve the riddle of God's existence. For, of course, God might be able to answer questions of creation, eternal life, good and evil, death, the existence of pain and suffering and everything else that no one has ever answered.

Thus I began reading *The Bible*.

Christmas came. The religious significance of the day seemed insincere, people just wanted a holiday, for how could God care whether or not we celebrated the birth of Christ? Christmas at our house was always pleasant. My mother and father would cook together for the feast, and we would eat in the dining room with a turkey, stuffing, cranberry sauce and sparkling cider in wine glasses. Come morning I would usually get clothing and books. The previous Christmas my gifts were a wool sweater, socks, some books, a down comforter, a thesaurus, and a tote bag. That Christmas I had only a couple small gifts under the tree, but in the stocking there was a set of keys. My parents told me to go to the garage, and there I found a green '73 Ford Pinto. The car was an insect, but I didn't care, it ran. I was very thankful, and told my parents so. The gift was a combined Christmas and birthday present, for my eighteenth birthday was on the tenth of January.

I spent the rest of the break reading and becoming indoctrinated by *The Bible's* eloquent prose, seeking serene locations in which to contemplate. My Pinto expanded and increased my haunts. I formulated views on heaven, hell, good, and evil, as a child would play war games with green army men.

One day in the middle of January, I was walking out of class with Dennis. He would be curious about what I did on weekends or after school, and he kept asking me if and when I'd be up for another party. He'd say, "So, Tarzan, when're you gonna come out of the jungle and hang with humanity?"

I'd reply, "When, of all possible choices, I have no other alternative."

Sometimes he'd say, "All right, Mr. Anti-social, there's a party this weekend at Derek's, babes and booze galore, whaddya say, you love hunter you?"

I'd shrug and grin.

That day, as we were walking out of class he questioned, "Whaddya think of Julie?"

"Who's Julie?"

"Second row, far right, long brown hair."

"Oh."

Dennis glided close to my side, "Now, I don't want you gettin' any ideas in your head, but word has it she's got eyes for you."

I nodded and twisted my lips as a response. We walked a couple more paces, as he, with open mouth, waited for a response. Finally he nudged me, "Well?"

I shrugged again and he stopped me, "Listen, Julie's got the hots for you, and she's gorgeous, any guy'd kill to go out with her. Not only that, but she's the type who'd like swingin' from trees with you, she's into nature and that stuff. Now if I were you I'd ask her out."

I stared at him.

He pressed, "Well, don't you think she's good looking?"

He patted me on the shoulder.

I said, "She's all right."

"All right?" Dennis spread his arms.

"Yeah, she's very pretty!"

Just then Julie passed us, she'd been walking behind the whole time, and she smiled at me in the fraction of a second that we made eye contact. I was startled as she walked down the hall.

Dennis slapped me, "Get on the ball, Paul, here's your chance. Go for it," and he left me stunned as I watched them both disappear in opposite directions down the hallway. Blood had rushed to my face, and I laughed at myself.

That evening my father called me into the living room. He and my mother were sitting on the couch, and I sat in a chair across from them.

My father began, "All right, Paul, I hope you've given some thought about what you're planning on doing after high school."

I was silent.

"Well?"

I said, "To be honest, I don't know."

He said, "Have you thought about any college that might interest you?"

"Ummm, nope."

"I see," my father turned and looked at my mother, who tipped her head slightly. He spoke, "We can send you pretty much anywhere. Think about it."

I glanced at my father, then my mother, who said, "You'd like college."

My father told me I should take the Scholastic Aptitude Test. I promised him I would. I took my parents for granted. To me, they were two people with whom I lived with. The meaning of life was more important, consuming me to the point where I regarded my parents as hosts.

That evening I did think about the future. Influenced by the styles of Descartes or Socrates, minus penetrating insight, I began a journal, written in first-person ignorant:

I am a philosopher. I have always been a philosopher, and now I realize this pursuit is mine. Philosophy means love of knowledge; I love knowledge. Love is a deep affection, and I have a deep affection for the attainment of knowledge. It is only fitting that I become a philosopher.

The first riddle I shall attempt to solve is the question of God's existence. This is crucial in determining whether morality exists, if justice exists, and, most importantly, what will happen when we die. I am reading *The Bible*, and it is very impressive, yet its meaning seems ambiguous. I am told only God can judge, but I must judge for myself as to the significance of *The Bible*. I can see I am in for a battle against deciphering contradiction. But *The Bible* says there are no contradictions, so it must come down to faith...

February began, and I was into the *New Testament*. There was a different feel to it, and I even laughed aloud once, when I read Matthew 19:24: "It is easier for a camel to go through the eye of a needle, than for a rich man to enter the kingdom of God." There was wit in this, but it could not be God's actual words, only those of a scribe of God who was influenced by God's power and wanted to add his own clever ideas into *The Bible*. *The Bible* was obviously written by men, and I set about the task of interpreting it.

I read Paul's epistles. One verse in particular explained something to me, 2 Timothy 3:16-17:

All scripture is given by inspiration of God, and is profitable for doctrine, for reproof, for correction, for instruction in righteousness:

That the man of God may be perfect, thoroughly furnished unto all good works.

There it was, it said *The Bible* was inspired by God, but not that it was the actual word of God. Also, in a way, it was a promise of perfection, attainment of the knowledge I was seeking.

One Saturday afternoon I walked out on the dock. There were no boats tied to the pier or anchored nearby, and no people, as well, not even a fisherman. It had rained earlier, and the wet wood slightly reflected the gray sky. I saw a figure walk out on the dock. It was Julie, with her red jacket and long, dark brown hair. When she was within fifty feet of me I ceased pretending I hadn't noticed her and turned to look at her, as I would feel sillier feigning obviousness to her presence. It was the least uncomfortable alternative. She smiled slightly with cute dimples, as she met my eyes. When she was a few feet away she said, "Hi, Paul."

"Hi," I could feel my tongue in my mouth, and didn't want to speak for fear of yammering and yawing.

"I saw you out here, so I thought I'd walk out and say hi," she smiled cautiously. I sensed she was uncomfortable, too.

"Oh, really," I felt more relaxed as I realized we were mutually nervous, "Well, hi."

She stood there, and as tense as I was I felt a magical surge rush through me. I asked, "So, uh, where do you live?"

She pointed to the other side of town, "I live there, in that blue house, with the deck hanging over the water."

"Oh, I see it. Yeah, that's a nice house."

She leaned against the railing and tossed her hair behind her, and breathed in, "I've always wanted to talk to you, you're so mysterious. What do you do with your time?"

"I think about things, and look at nature. The ocean, the trees," I was beginning to feel comfortable, "Want to walk on the beach? I'll show you my house."

"Sure."

As we walked down the dock, she hopped and skipped ahead of me in the mild wind as her hair danced behind, and as I stepped behind her I was still looking into her pretty brown eyes. She waited for me at the end of the dock, and when I reached her I pointed to a trail that went to the beach. She stepped down it, and I followed her. The blue sky was trying to break through the clouds, there were a couple hours of daylight left, the seagulls were singing and screeching, and mussels and barnacles crunched under our feet.

Ahead of me, she yelled through stiff breeze, "I love walking on the beach!"

She jumped from stone to stone to log to stone to log, and I followed. Finally, she found a log and sat down. I went over and sat on the same log, three feet from her.

"It's really strange that you came out on the dock," I said.
"Why?"

"I don't know, it seems like destiny."

"Oh," her hands were in the pockets of her coat, "Well, it was destiny that you were out there."

"Yeah," I shrugged, "What do you do all day?"

"Everything. I dance and sing in our house when no one's around, or even when they are. I play with Brandon, my little brother, he's three years old. He's such a cutie. I like to watch the rain fall on the water as I eat oatmeal cookies in our living room. I'm never bored, there's always something to do." She stood and stretched, "C'mon, show me your house."

When we were beneath my house I pointed to it, two hundred feet above us. We walked backwards to get a better view, but the tide didn't give us much room. I said, "So there it is. You can barely see the roof. My bedroom's on the second floor overlooking the water." I pointed to the triangular top of our house as it peeked out from the evergreens. "There's a path along the top of the cliff. It goes all the way down, and I sit up there and look over the ocean. An eagle sometimes flies over and about, and I think of what it must be like to be him."

She looked at the bluff, the madronas at the edge and the evergreens standing above them, and said, "Your house must be wonderful."

"Yeah, it's not too bad."

She asked me if I was an only child, and I told her I was.

"Aren't you lonely? Being the only kid?"

"Well, I am if loneliness is the state of being alone, but I've never really been bothered by it." The sun was setting behind clouds and we could see translucent light thinning out and slipping over the horizon. Julie told me about her family, her siblings, and the fact she had lived in California previous to Washington.

We walked back towards the dock, and as we did we brushed against one another and she slid her hand into mine and wrapped her fingers around my fingers. I'd never held anyone's hand before, and it was astonishing how all I could think about was this hand, smaller than mine and very warm, in my hand. The warmth spread all over me.

There we were, at the dock facing one another, still holding hands. We stared in each other's eyes. And we kept a steady gaze between us until she said, "If you don't let go, I won't be able to go home."

"I know."

She laughed, and pulled her hands away. Placing them around my neck she kissed me on the lips once. "Would you like to meet me here tomorrow?"

"Sure."

"How does four o'clock sound?"

It sounded fine, her arms were still around me, and we kissed again, "My parents are expecting me, so I'll say good-bye. 'Til tomorrow, then."

I watched her walk into town until she was out of sight. I felt light, I was made of Styrofoam, warm as an oven, soft as pudding. I never knew what a kiss could do.

Late that evening I was in my room reading *The Bible*. Much of *The Bible* I found difficult, even incomprehensible, I felt that simply by reading *The Bible* I would be able to say I had read, understood, and had gained meaning from it. Nevertheless, there were some parts that caught my full attention. Both Ecclesiastics and Proverbs were perfect for moments when I was in the mood to muse over an aphorism, and I came across Proverbs 18:22, "Whoso findeth a woman findeth a good thing, and obtaineth favour of the Lord." Of course, I thought - destiny! This was guidance. All at once divine bliss came to me, the culmination of God, love, and now Julie. An incredible wave of ecstasy rushed through me and filled me completely, tears almost flowed from my eyes, and then the moment left. But I had never felt so refreshed, so good, and my faith had been born. There was a sense of purity and righteousness within, and at that moment I was convinced that God existed and *The Bible* was true, showing me the ways of God, and Julie and I would fall in love, and the eagle would fly about forever, cold saltwater would dash and foam against the shore, branches would blow in the wind, and in my room with a seascape in motion I slept peacefully.

The following afternoon I met Julie with anticipation. She was wearing a sweatshirt and sweatpants along with her red

24

jacket. Her hair was in a ponytail, and she still smiled with dimples and pretty brown eyes. I never considered how being in someone's presence could be pleasurable. She asked me if I had any special plans, and I suggested we go to my place, and then we could drive my car. She didn't know I had a car, and was mildly surprised.

As we walked to my house we held hands. When we went inside I introduced Julie to my parents, and showed her our living room with its view. I brought her upstairs to my room and I stood by my window telling her how I spent time looking out at the Pacific. As we stood I took both her hands, brought them to my face, and kissed them, and then I kissed her on the lips. We slid our arms around each other and kissed a couple times, and then we held each other tighter and kissed fully, and I experienced the sensation of soft tongue upon tongue.

I mentioned we should go, and we went downstairs and to my car parked in the driveway. We drove slowly to the coast, winding in and out and through trees, and ending up at a boat landing I had discovered on a jaunt a few days earlier. On the right side of us the trees went to the logs and beach, which stretched far, and on the other side a cliff rose, a house was a little ways up it. We sat on a log near my car, and played with pebbles, talked about hermit crabs and seals, pretended to smoke the cigar-shaped driftwood, and kissed and petted until the sun went down. Then we went back inside the car, as the night air chilled. We made out, and we wrapped completely around each other, legs and arms entwined. She was breathing loud and kissing my neck and ears. Her breasts and hips were pressed against my body, and we were both in the passenger seat. She whispered, "Wouldn't it be nice if we could spend a whole night together?"

"Yeah, very nice," I agreed, thinking I could hold her endlessly. The illusion of forever.

In the car, with the window cracked, I said, "You know what I like about a girl?"

She glanced at me.

I continued, "I like a girl who appreciates scenery."

She said, "And I like a guy who likes a girl who appreciates scenery."

I quipped, "Well, I like a girl who likes a guy who likes a girl who appreciates scenery."

We stayed there, fogging the windows, until it had been dark for quite a while, and then I took her to her house. I parked in front and she said, "Paul, Tolo's coming up, it's a week from Saturday. Would you go with me?"

Tolo was a Valentine's Day dance at our high school in which the girls asked the guys out. It was a semi-formal affair. I had never been to a dance.

"I guess."

"You guess?"

"I guess I'll go."

She kissed me, "Great, it'll be a lot of fun," and she kissed me again,

"You're cute, you know that?"

I'd never been complimented before. I said, "I didn't know guys could be cute, if anyone's cute it's you."

We kissed a little longer, and then she left, with me floating in the car.

That night, when I was in my bedroom, my father called me downstairs and into the kitchen. My mother was in the living room playing the piano, and my father sat on a stool and asked, "So, have you thought about college?"

"Well-" and I stopped, for I hadn't given a lot of thought to the issue. I had signed up to take the S.A.T., however, and I told my father that.

"We can afford to send you anywhere, even Seton Hall," which was my parents' alma mater. " Pretty soon you'll be out of high school, and I'm all for the idea of people wandering in and out of trees and along beaches, but you can't do that in the real world."

"What's the real world?"

"It's a harsh world, Paul. It's every man for himself, and you'll find out that you'll have to fend for yourself. You're not going to have a home and allowance and food all paid for, like you have now. You may or may not realize how sheltered you are, but your life is only a slice of what it's like to be in the real world. You've never seen true suffering. This place is heaven compared to a lot of places, and someday you'll have to provide for yourself, and maybe a family. A college education will make your life much easier. Think about it."

I pursed my lips for a moment, and then replied, "I'm not too sure I need to see the sickness of the world to appreciate my life, and, to tell you the truth, I'd rather not. Hey, I'm all for expanding my horizons, but I don't see how college is the only way."

I told him I would give serious thought to my future, and I went upstairs.

My parents. Would I ever talk to them about this or that? Julie? Or even God? That my parents gave me an allowance, and a place to live, was taken for granted. That my parents gave me love went almost unnoticed.

That evening I read in my *Bible* with its flaking leather cover and thin pages. Lying in bed I finally put away the book and stared out the window. Yes, I realized, I'm okay, I have a comfortable life, I should appreciate it more. And I can still dream.

During the week I spent a lot of time with Julie. I only had the one class with her, but every day we ate lunch together, and in the evening we usually found something to do. She came over a couple times, and one night after she left and I'd returned from taking her home my father said, "Paul, Paul. You've finally discovered girls. I just wanted to tell you I'm happy for you."

He was standing in the living room, my mother was on the couch and he put his hand on her shoulder, "How does it feel to have a girlfriend?"

"Ummm, she's not really a girlfriend."

My father smiled, "Then what is she?"

"Hmmm," I stood there and reflected; when she smiles it is joy to be at the receiving end, her presence makes me aware that I once was alone, in class I stare at her, a diversion from education. I said, "I guess she is a girlfriend."

They laughed quietly and exchanged a knowing look as I left the room.

During school Dennis said to me, "So, you made the move, huh?" He nudged me, "You're not as out of it as I thought."

I grinned somewhat as a reply.

I met her parents and family. Once, when I had to wait for Julie, I stood in their living room and watched a commercial on their television set. It was a cereal commercial, frosted something or other, and Julie's younger brother and sister sat glued to the insipid box. I realized what an influence television was.

Julie and I drove around frequently, seeking scenery. Sometimes we'd hike down a trail or on a beach. My relationship with God and Julie were running parallel, but they hadn't met yet. The topic of God had never been talked about between us, but once, when we drove by the town's Catholic church she commented, "Why do Christians prefer to have a fancy church to pray in? Why don't they spend all that money on the poor?"

I shrugged as an answer. I wasn't sure what to think about her views on God, which I didn't know yet. I thought all it took for someone to believe in Christianity was to plant the seed of knowledge in them. If she was Christian, great, if not then it couldn't be that difficult of a matter to show her the way. Besides, I agreed with her about church. Church, it seemed to me, was a show, a pompous display, a social gathering. When I had gone the reverend hadn't radiated much humor or warmth but rather a cold, austere perception of the wonders and love of God. Faith should exude beneficence, and I didn't get that impression at church.

In those moments when we kissed and made out, in my car or in my room, our hands would find ways to sneak under clothing, the sensation of skin on skin was titillating. I would feel the small of her back, her waist, her shoulders, and the side of her torso, but I never touched her breasts except through clothing when our chests pressed against one another. I didn't think it would be proper to touch her breasts yet, I was well aware of my virginity, and thought that to lose it was a gradual, step by step process culminating in marriage.

One evening, after being with Julie, I was in my room reading the *New Testament*, and I became intoxicated with the idea reiterated throughout the Gospels, "Seek, and ye shall find; ask, and ye shall receive." This I believed, and thus I became another of countless souls who have thought this verse actually meant; seek, and ye shall find, ask, and ye shall receive. And all I asked for was guidance. I prayed: God, guide me. I thought of asking for Julie, but I didn't, because I thought there were some things better left to fate.

On Valentine's Day, a Thursday, I gave Julie flowers. We sat parked on this lookout at the base of a bluff, and we were kissing in the passenger seat. About thirty feet below us was the ocean splattering against rocks, shadows of trees surrounded us, and behind us the cliff rose perhaps a hundred feet. This was our favorite lookout as it was secluded, and we could hug and kiss and nuzzle for a meantime. As we were making out she put her hand over my crotch and felt my erection. She rubbed gently and said, "After Tolo we can stay at my friend Katie's house. Her parents are gone for the weekend, so we can finally sleep together."

"No kidding, I can't wait," I felt that was the right thing to say. She stopped rubbing and smiled, perhaps she saw the befuddlement in my eyes.

I remember this moment. Of all the time spent with Julie this is one of my most vivid memories. I was bubbling with what I considered happiness. I didn't think anything could go wrong, and although things went well for a while, my confusion began to grow from this point. An adult expects the unexpected, so when it happens there is surprise, but the shock is greater when one is younger. A youth is rarely prepared for the unexpected.

Julie and I decided to dress formally for Tolo. I wore a rented tuxedo, she wore a red satin dress, her hair was in a French braid. Her dress didn't cover her shoulders. She looked gorgeous. She usually wore little make up, and that night she had on a noticeable amount, but it accentuated her features. Her parents took pictures of us as we stood in front of my Pinto. I opened the passenger door for her, sauntered over to my side and we departed as her parents still shot an occasional flash at us.

As we were driving I said, "I cant believe it. You look so beautiful tonight'"

"You're a pretty sharp looking fella, yourself."

She kissed me on the lips and giggled as she saw my expression, "It's cherry, like it?"

Our first stop was a restaurant, an inn made of logs and stone, overlooking the sea. It had a colonial, antiquated feel to it. We had a window booth with a view of the ocean and some rocks jutting out into the water. The booth, with its high backrest of cedar, and its velvet, scarlet cushions, created a cozy and intimate atmosphere; with infrequent interruptions by the waitress.

Julie said, "Two weeks ago we barely knew each other."

"Yeah."

"That's so weird, isn't it?" she sat, and rubbed her hand on the smooth round wood underneath the sill, "And now we're getting to know each other, it's so exciting."

"Yeah."

"And isn't it strange how we spent about half a year together in Math class without noticing each other."

"Yeah, real strange." I was smiling and looking at her throughout.

She put her hand on mine, "But I'm lying, I noticed you. You were so mysterious. I was so scared to talk to you, you're so quiet, I didn't know if you were shy or stuck up. And to think that you're such a sweetie."

"Well, I-", but I didn't know what to say, and let her continue.

"In a way, we can thank Dennis."

"Dennis?"

"Yeah, he suggested that I should talk to you."

"Hmmm."

"He said you were an all right guy."

"He did, huh?" That Dennis. I wondered, "Just out of curiosity, did you overhear that conversation of ours in the hall after class that day?"

"What conversation?" She rolled her eyes.

"You know, the one where I blurted out that I thought you were pretty."

"Oh, that one," she laughed. "Actually, I heard you say someone was pretty but I wasn't sure if it was me you were talking about."

"Right."

"But Dennis dropped a hint to me."

I grinned.

30

Her fingers played with mine, and she said, "Yeah, if Dennis hadn't told me it'd be all right to talk to you I don't know if I'd ever have gotten the nerve to walk up to you on the dock that day. And I know you never would've come up to me."

Leaning back, I said, "I mean this, I'm glad you did. Real glad, you wouldn't know how glad even. You're right, I don't know how to talk to people, and I'd never have approached you. You know, I never would have guessed going out with a girl would be so nice."

She was holding my hand, and she pulled it up to her mouth and kissed it. We kissed each other's hands, made silly eyes at one another, and spoke in romantic banter, and somewhere in between infatuation the waitress came and went, came and went, taking our order, serving it, taking it away, half-eaten. We ordered dessert, and fed each other forkfuls. Afterwards we took a walk on the stone path behind the restaurant, and the slight breeze blew Julie's dress, flapping it around her body.

We went to the dance, had our pictures taken, and Julie even succeeded in getting me out on the floor. We danced the slow ones, and even a couple of fast ones. I did all right with the slow songs, but the fast ones made me feel like a boulder lodged in river rapids. Dennis was there with his date, and he winked at me, but we didn't get a chance to talk. Julie and Katie whispered things to each other when the dance was finishing, and we departed to Katie's house.

It was well after midnight when we arrived at Katie's house, a one-story rambler a couple miles inland, on a farm surrounded by woods. There was a barn, and a pasture and some livestock. Julie and I were the first to arrive, and barely had time to cuddle before Katie and her date, Rob, came. Rob was a familiar face, and that was it. Julie introduced me to the pair. Katie, with blonde, bobbed hair, was constantly adjusting a strap of her dress and Rob, with his crewcut, didn't know whether he should leave his shirt tucked in or not. Finally he took off his jacket and untucked his shirt and went into the kitchen .

Katie said to me, "It's your fault."

I was taken aback, and after Katie saw my reply was speechlessness, she said, "Because of you I haven't done anything with Julie for two weeks."

Julie interjected, "Like you didn't disappear right after you started going out with Rob."

"At least I called you every once in a while and told you what's going on. You just vanished off the face of the earth."

Julie put her arm around me, "I guess Paul's to blame," and she kissed me on the cheek.

I grinned, "Uh, I'd say I should get the credit, not the blame." Everyone laughed.

Rob returned and placed four wine glasses on the table. Then he filled them with champagne. If they had asked me if I wanted any I would have refused. I had told Julie of my one experience with alcohol, and had implied, although probably ambiguously, that it was a one-time experience. I didn't say anything, and even took a taste of the bittersweet, bubbling water.

Julie and Katie conversed, while Rob and I sat listening. Finally Rob spoke to me, after he had finished a glass of champagne and was pouring himself another.

"Paul, tell me about yourself." His words were spoken slowly, and clearly, as if he was making extra sure he'd be understood.

I said, "There's not much to tell, I go to school, and when the day's over I go home."

"Is that it?"

"Not entirely, I read some, wander some, and now I hang with Julie some."

"Hmmm, whaddya read?"

"Just stuff."

"Stuff, could you be more vague?" Rob was sitting in a chair across from me and Julie, with Katie in his lap.

I told Rob, "You know, anything, whatever's lying around."

Rob nodded, and then said, "You ever thought about playing ball?"

"Ball?"

"Yeah, football, basketball, baseball. Ball."

"Not really."

"Why not? You're a big guy, linebacker material. It's a blast, I tell ya."

"Terry Collins?"

Terry was this guy with long hair and a leather jacket. He hung out with a mangy crowd. This was too much. I acted as if I didn't care, even though I was sizzling. I couldn't believe it. I had told Julie, once, that I could never think anything bad about her. I was wrong. My opinion of her lowered considerably, I called the grapes sour, and didn't want to have anything to do with her. In class I pretended not to know her.

As days passed, I began to feel more relaxed. There is a discipline, a determination, an iron precision and straight-forwardness that is the result of self-righteousness. I believed what I was doing was correct. I may not have had wisdom, experience, and understanding, but at least I had ignorance. Maybe I will never reach this level of confidence again, one usually needs ignorance of ignorance to have firm convictions, or, of course, compassion and understanding. I, along with the majority of people who have firm convictions, had the former, and the state the world is in is indicative of this .

Occasionally I thought it would be a good idea to talk to my father, just talk to him about what was troubling me. Maybe it was Julie, or the uncertainty of God contradicted by my certainty of following the path to God, and maybe it was something related but something I missed. But I never could, I would walk into the house and see him sitting at the dining table scrawling notes on a piece of paper, or munching an apple, or maybe I would hear him working on his lathe in the garage, and I would say nothing. Or, if I did happen to say something it was about schoolwork or weather, or chores, and little else. I told myself I wanted no advice from anyone. Now that I look back I'm sure I was filled with doubt, but I never considered myself possessing the quantity that I had. And so I indoctrinated myself with my own ideas; that I was right, and I would patiently sit about waiting to talk to God, and gain inspiration and guidance. I told myself that what I would have to do would be like crawling into a hollow log and simply waiting until God came to me. My only occupation would be prayer exercised with faith and patience.

Julie, I would reflect, was temptation averted. A little fish thrown in the way of my great plans, and she would return to the mass of nameless humanity while I strove for the nameless. I was a sinewed and tethered chunk of pride and insecurity. I thought my peers more ignorant that I had ever considered them before, and I never had been one to give my peers much credit. I wrote more. I saw gaps in my own knowledge, and I expected them to be filled by God, and reading *The Bible*. Yet I didn't know how large these gaps were and how they can never be filled. The only way they would disappear was to stop calling them gaps.

The school year was nearing its end, school spirit surrounded me, and I trudged along. I have cried, literally, to think of the youth I was. Of the things I missed. Love.

Although I repressed my feelings for Julie I still cared for her. If she had ever told me shed missed me and wanted to come back into my life I would have been filled with delight, and perhaps this is part of the reason why I became so engrossed in religion, so I could be sidetracked, although I cannot say for sure. However, I continued to elude her presence unless it was unavoidable. In the last week of school, I ran into her in the hall, we were alone, and made eye contact. She stopped, so I did the same. For a moment it appeared we wouldn't say anything and would disperse.

But she said, "Paul, why're you being such a butt?"

"I don't know what you're talking about."

"C'mon, you never talk to me, it's like I don't exist. I wish you'd try and be friends."

"Friends. I am your friend."

"How can you say that? You act like you hate me or something. I just look at you and you turn to stone."

But she said, "Paul, why're you being such a butt?"

"I don't know what you're talking about."

"C'mon, you never talk to me, it's like I don't exist. I wish you'd try and be friends."

"Friends. I am your friend."

"How can you say that? You act like you hate me or something. I just look at you and you turn to stone."

"I guess I have things on my mind."

She leaned against the wall and shook her head slowly, "I'm sorry we can't be friends."

50

"I'm sorry, too. I think about you a lot."

"You do?"

"Yes, I pray for you."

Hearing this Julie's expression turned sour, "Don't bother, maybe someday you'll see I don't need it." And she walked down the hall. But I had meant it as a compliment, a yearning; although, I suppose, I also meant I had prayed for her well-being.

During the week of graduation, I had minimal contact with teachers and classmates. Some teachers asked me what I was doing after school, and they seemed somewhat surprised I wasn't going to further my education. As for the ceremony, I saw no need to celebrate this ritual of entering the world. I prepared to live the life of an ascetic. I wrote in my journal, still, and every once in a while I wrote a poem, praising nature or describing an emotion. Before I had written primarily philosophy and devotional prose.

So graduation wafted by, my parents attended, and, overall, it was an unexceptional scene. At the post-graduation ceremony, I was approached by Julie before I had time to leave, and she gave me her annual to sign. I scrawled "Paul Taylor" on the back page, gave it to her, and departed.

On this note, I began life after high school. In the morning the shadows of trees snuck through my window pane, the sun was east and not visible but pink and lavender smoke skimmed the horizon and started my days. My parents didn't seem to mind too much the fact I wasn't going to school. My father would sometimes ask me if I'd heard anything from God. One time, after I told him I was still waiting but there was plenty of time, he said, "Jesus was a carpenter, he didn't just sit on his butt before becoming a servant of God."

"Yeah, well, if I'm not meant to sit on my butt then I'm sure I'll receive a sign. I'll do whatever feels right."

"And lounging about like a bump on a log feels right?"

"So far," I replied. Of course, looking back, I'm sure my father had a bit of chagrin towards my arrogance, which I never considered. I assumed he was patient towards my quest.

He told me, "I really can't see why you won't talk to a

preacher. I'm sure you can find one who's wise and can give you some advice. It can't hurt. "

"I'm sure that's true, but what good can advice do? I'm determined to wait, regardless."

"Boy, you're stubborn. Tell me, what makes you think that you, of all people, will get this sign from God? You certainly need something to get you going, but I think if you're waiting to talk to God you'll have a long wait. And you're not going to be able to wait here all your life."

"Well, I'll worry about that when the time comes."

"What you say goes completely past me. You don't make sense, you really don't."

"I don't think anyone can understand what I'm thinking."

My father nodded his head a little, pursed his lips, "I'll buy that, but I don't think you understand what anyone else is thinking, and, for that matter, do you understand what you, yourself, are thinking?"

In July I fasted for seven days and nights. One hundred and sixty-eight hours. I drank water and that was my only source of nourishment. Jesus fasted for forty days and nights, I contemplated as I began, seven seemed trivial. The seven days took a long time. A very long time. I look back at those seven days, and I know it seemed like forever while I was experiencing them, but what do I remember?

I wrote and read little, the majority of time was spent sleeping or lying about wishing I could sleep. I counted each moment, each hour. One thirty-one hours-to-go ... ninety hours-to-go ... only twenty-nine hours left. It was no fun. I had narcissistic moments, commending myself for the feat of devotion. As well, I had a spell or two of pure thought induced by prayer which further reinforced my faith. These moments filled me with an inexplicable ecstasy, a hope that deep down inside I could do it, that somewhere inside me there was love that could be harnessed; a power of goodness flickering in my soul and giving me assurance. I lost seventeen pounds, I fainted twice, and only wrote a couple brief entries in my journal. When I slept I couldn't remember my dreams. I didn't feel any closer to God, but I did feel further from everything else, so, in effect, God was all there was. When it was over I felt very pleased, it was an accomplishment of sorts. It reiterated my beliefs.

After a feast at midnight of the seventh day, I slept soundly and resigned myself to what possibly might be a long wait. I began to read works aside from *The Bible* more often. And every once in a while I would think about Julie. I had gotten over the hurt and was able to look and consider that maybe I was at fault. Maybe I could have tried to talk to her, and at least make an attempt to be friends. I wished I had spoken to her with some friendliness, and had signed her annual with more than a signature. What was troubling was that as I slowly confronted the fact that I loved her I realized I had done little about it. I realized that although God was important, there were other things in life that had importance.

During that summer I spent a lot of time driving around the coast and inland, taking hikes all over, along with reading and writing. I spent even less time with my parents than I had during the school year.

When September came I was in town, near Julie's house, and on the spur of the moment I decided to go there. I knocked on the door and her mother invited me inside, immediately telling me Julie had already departed to California for college. She was to attend Stanford. I chose not to go in and told her to pass my greetings on, and she told me Julie was planning on returning over Christmas break.

It was odd not to be in school in the fall. Even though I wasn't social, I was used to being in the midst of people at this time. Occasionally I would feel truant during the day. This lack of interaction with people for an extended period of time took some getting used to. I felt bottled up inside my journal. I began to talk to my parents more.

There are elements in ones surroundings that go unnoticed until they finally penetrate the senses of one's consciousness with full force. As I sat in my bedroom one evening I became intently aware of extraordinary music coming from downstairs. I left my room and went to the piano, asking my mother what she was playing.

"It's Mozart."

"It's beautiful," I said.

"Yes," she turned, "Mozart wrote perfect music."

"What else do you play?"

My mother glanced at her sheet music, "I play the classical composers, but sometimes I just play what I feel."

"Well, I wanted to tell you it's really good, and keep it up," I said, then realizing the latter comment was unnecessary.

My mother smiled in gratitude, and I stepped out of the room.

I decided I would learn to play. I'd taken band in junior high, and music theory seemed simple enough. Infrequently, in the past, I had tinkled on our piano, and I could play a few simple melodies, but I knew if I spent hours practicing I could occupy my time more during the cold days that approached.

I played and played. Sometimes my mother and I would compete for use of the piano, and I would have to patiently wait for my turn. She would give me advice, "Learn to use the pedals correctly," "Practice with each hand so they are equally nimble and be able to play melody and harmony with each hand," or "It's to your advantage to read music. The great composers can teach you a lot." I never did figure out how to read music and play simultaneously, I could methodically translate written notes into music but I never became adept at this skill. My time was filled, I had music, literature, *The Bible,* and my wait for God to lead me to my inevitable destiny.

By Christmas break I was beginning to feel comfortable at the piano. I was a lifetime away from the excellence of my mother, but I could enjoy the piano in greater leaps. Now I knew that in nine months I'd have to have a solution, and I was sure some plan or direction would arise by then. I was gracious toward my parents, and helped out around the house whenever possible, without being asked to. Inwardly I thanked them for their shelter and love, but I was still unable to converse with them to any significant degree.

A week before Christmas I called Julie, she was home and somewhat surprised to hear from me. I asked her if we could have a talk and she said it would be fine. I drove my Pinto to her house and met Julie at the door. She asked me what made me call.

"I guess I miss you. I'd like to be friends."

"That's sweet," she hugged me and we took a drive to a boat landing near the dock. It was raining and very windy, so we stayed in the car and looked out at an ocean in turmoil.

I didn't know what to say, so I asked, "Well, how's school?"

"It's great, it really is, you'd love it. Class is so 'lax, and you're treated like an adult. You can choose the subjects you want to take. It's an extension of high school, but more fun."

I nodded my head slightly.

"So, what have you been up to?" Julie wanted to know.

I thought for a moment, "Oh, nothing much, I'm just hangin' around." She didn't say anything, so I kept talking, "Julie, I've realized that I acted wrong. I could've been more understanding towards you. I mean, I'm still Christian, but I agree with you, I think. It's wrong to send someone to hell. I blew it, you were right in breaking up with me."

"Yeah, you were really a dick."

"I guess. And when I heard you were seeing Terry right after we broke up I was mad. I wanted to erase you."

Julie puffed her cheeks and sighed, "Terry was an asshole. He only wanted one thing, and he didn't get it. That was that."

Her explanation of the scene made me feel better about that episode, I said, "You know, it's taken time for me to see what a fool I'd been. I just wanted to apologize to you."

"Oh," Julie put her hand on my shoulder, "That's really nice."

I didn't know whether or not I should try to kiss her, so I just stared at her and breathed deeply. My attraction to her had never died, nor had my love. I wanted to kiss her. I moved close to her and grabbed her hand with mine, and gradually put my lips against hers, "Do you mind?"

"No."

And we started kissing. It was strange, almost too strange, to be kissing her. It was definitely unexpected, and it was pleasant and soothing. Indeed, it was a sweet sensation to recapture and feel again the familiar and gentle motion of our lips and tongues in contact. We embraced, after a long period of kissing, and I said, "I know you're not up for long, but it'd be nice to go out a couple times, for old times' sake."

"Yeah, it would."

Julie pressed her forehead against my shoulder for a while and we were silent as we looked out my rain-splattered window at the night.

She whispered, "You know it'll be temporary, I'm only here for the break. It wouldn't mean anything, for now."

"I have no expectations, well, I know for now that it's just for now."

We kissed a little more, and Julie asked, "So, how deep are you into your God trip?"

"I'm a little more mellow about it. My strength is still strong, but I realize there's a lot to life, and I know so little. As I said, I no longer am sure about heaven and hell, but I'm sure whatever God's plan is that it's fair."

"I'm glad." Julie gave me a peck on the cheek.

"Me too. I thought you might've forgotten me by now."

Julie laughed, "Of course not. I like you, I've always had a thing for you. You're such a cutie. You're tender and you're not out for sex like so many guys. I can really talk to you."

I said, "Yup, I really blew it."

"No you didn't."

We didn't stay much longer as she had to go home and be with her parents. I mused at my desk as I looked out my window later that evening. It was almost inconceivable that Julie would return into my life with such ease. As for my journal, and such remarks as 'Julie was temptation averted', they were forgotten.

I discovered my feelings for Julie were not just an excitable fire or a fervent desire, my passion was also warmth all over and inside me. Thus a hope returned, and although I was slightly wary I wasn't concerned too much about what would happen between Julie and me, things would work themselves out.

The next day Julie and I drove out to one of our favorite places near the beach. Julie wanted to hear my reasons for not furthering my education, and when I explained the role God played in my life and how I was waiting for God to tell me what to do she listened patiently.

When I finished she gave a cute giggle, "Has anyone told you you're nuts?"

"My father has a couple times. But I have a feeling he'll be real proud of me if I'm successful."

Her head shook back and forth, "You're a fruitcake, you're bananas, cuckoo."

"You know, Julie, you're the only friend I've got."

She sighed gently and put her arms around me. We hugged for a long time, and I said, "Julie, I love you, I've never told you this but I think I've always loved you. I can't help it, I just do."

"Paul," she pushed herself away and held both my hands in hers. And then she pulled herself to me, "Paul, I love you too, I don't know if it's in the same way. But I'm young, and I've been in love, and I'm leaving the day after New Year's."

"Can I hope?"

"Yes," she whispered.

Christmas rolled by, I was given more books, clothes, and a pair of sheepskin seat covers for my Pinto. I spent time with Julie whenever possible, and she split her time between myself, her family, and friends.

For New Year's Eve Julie had the option of going to a party with Katie or spending time with me. I told her she could go to the party if she wished. To my surprise she said she preferred to spend time with me, for it was the last chance she would have of seeing me for a while. However, I was mulling over the possibility of driving down to California to be with her, and I had not mentioned this idea to Julie. I reasoned I had nothing to gain by staying in Washington, and could lounge and wait for God just as easily in California, so why not go down? If it didn't turn out I could come back. I hadn't considered the financial aspect of it.

So on New Year's Eve Julie came over and we saw the year change as a half moon was reflected on a surprisingly calm sheet of dark blue. My parents had taken a trip to Victoria, British Columbia, and would not return until the following day. We had the house to ourselves.

I played the piano, Julie made hot chocolate, we counted down the New Year together, the Christmas tree was still up with its dancing array of colored lights, and we set candles around the room and cuddled on the couch. I asked her when she was expected home.

"Tomorrow, my parents think I'm staying at Katie's."

"No kidding," I said, and after we conversed a bit we went by candlelight upstairs and into my room. The house was toaster warm, and in no time Julie and I were in underpants lying on the bed, under the soft light, a single candle gently played along the contours of her naked breasts and belly.

"Are you still a virgin?" Julie grinned.

"What do you think?"

"Just asking," Julie nibbled my ear, "You wouldn't want to lose your virginity, would you?"

"Eventually."

"How 'bout now?"

"I definitely want you to be my first," I said thoughtfully, "But I don't know, I mean, it'd mean a lot to me and I haven't really thought about it yet. I'd like to have sex with one girl for the rest of my life."

Julie kissed my cheek, "You're so different. I respect that. Well, we can still sleep together."

"Yeah we can."

We kissed more and more and pressed our almost naked bodies to each other, and then I said, "Julie, what would you think if I came down to California? Just for a while, maybe, and if I like it I'll stay and if not I'll leave."

Julie stared at the ceiling, "I don't think it's a good idea."

"Why not? I mean, I want to be with you."

"It just can't work out like that, I've got school and things to do, I'm too busy to have a relationship right now."

"Julie, what if I wanted to go? How terrible can it be?"

Julie shook her head, "Paul, it's not a good idea. I have friends and a different life down there. It wouldn't work."

"It's worth a shot, at least. It's really been enjoyable these last two weeks, and it'd be me taking a chance. You'd be going to school."

Julie rolled a half turn away and lay on her side, facing me. She spoke slowly, "Paul, I'm gonna tell you. I didn't want to, but I have to. I'm seeing someone down there."

"A boyfriend?"

"Yeah, sorta, I mean, it's cool. There's no commitment, but we enjoy hangin' out with each other. I know you won't understand."

"A boyfriend," I stared at the ceiling.

"I'm sorry. Really, He's not a real boyfriend. I mean, if he was then I wouldn't have kissed you or anything, but we do hang out together."

"Well," I gritted my, teeth. Nothing was said for a moment. Finally, I asked, "So you thought you could just not tell me and go home and everything would be okay?"

"Yeah, I thought we could have some harmless fun. You enjoyed messing around, didn't you? I think romance is neat and I like your company, and what we did was fun. Don't you think so?"

"And you would've slept with me?"

"Paul, I feel really bad, I didn't want you to find out," she ran her finger tips up and down my arms.

I said, "Yeah, oh well. Here we are. I guess it's not surprising that you'd meet a guy sooner or later. It's just that, well, I feel deceived."

"I'm sorry. I'm so sorry. I'll never do it again."

"Let's just go to sleep," I said slowly.

She nestled against me and apologized again and said, "I hope you understand."

"I don't understand. You would have slept with me. It would've meant a lot to me, and you wouldn't even be around."

"I have different views about sex."

"I'll say."

"I'm sorry."

"It's okay, let's just go to sleep."

She wrapped herself around me.

I put my arms around her and said resignedly to the night, "I guess I still love you."

She squeezed me.

So we spent the night together underneath the sheet, listening to the wind blow through the trees. Melancholy enveloped me, and I didn't know what love or anything was. The next day we said our good-byes with a hug and a kiss. She said she'd call me when she returned from California. We exchanged addresses, but never wrote. The first time Julie and I split I felt indignant. This time I felt like a dope.

One day, in January after my nineteenth birthday, I decided I would take my father's suggestion and talk to a preacher. I drove to a church in town, it was a Sunday evening, and the doors were unlocked so I walked inside. There was a great room filled with pews in front of me, and on my right was a hall. I walked down, and into a room that looked like it served as a banquet or meeting place. There was no one there. I walked out and back down the hall. This time I noticed an open door with a man inside sitting at a desk. I asked him if he knew where I could find the reverend and he introduced himself. I didn't recognize him so I assumed he was new. His name was Reverend Martin.

I shook hands with him and he invited me to sit down.

He swiveled on his chair and turned to me, putting on a pair of glasses, "So, what can I do for you?"

"I'd like to talk to someone about God."

"Well, okay, then you came to the right place. Is there any particular aspect of God you'd like to talk about?"

His office was nicely furnished, with his leather upholstered chair, lacquered maple desk, and the expected *Bible*. On the wall was a picture of Jesus with his disciples, and The Beatitude's and The Lord's Prayer in a frame. Reverend Martin gave me an impression of friendliness, and I was instantly comfortable with this short, slightly plump man. The wrinkles on his face appeared to come from laughing, not frowning.

I explained how I wished to receive guidance from God, that I'd read *The Bible*, and been touched by God and had felt His presence. I told him I felt most comfortable waiting for God to direct me to my destination.

He said, "Have you thought about a Christian college?"

"Yeah, I just don't know."

"There are some great schools you could attend, and they have missions where you can go to a poor, underdeveloped country and educate them and spread the love of God."

"Uh huh, but right now I don't have an urgent desire to do that."

60

"Well, what do you want?"

"I want my doubt to be erased."

He leaned back, "You feel you lack faith?"

"No, I believe, but I need more than that. I don't feel right simply putting myself in God's hands and going off to start my life."

"What would make you feel right, then?"

I mused, "To talk to God. To feel his presence and assurance that I was doing the right thing."

"If you follow the Word of God, and obey Him and Christ, then you are doing the right thing. There are many ways to serve God. It sounds like you're putting your fate in God's hand, and while God determines your fate, you, also, must determine your fate."

I nodded.

He continued, "You're young, you want to know God, and it will take time. I'm sixty-three and I still don't know much about God or life, but I know about the things that matter. Surround yourself with God and love is sure to come. Pray and submit to God, but also be a responsible individual."

"Yeah, but it's too easy to say I have faith and that my worries shall be erased. For example, I don't see any purpose in suffering and death. And then to have judgment and heaven and hell at the end doesn't make sense. Why are people sent to hell just because they don't believe? It seems unfair."

"God is just. You have to put faith in that. He will judge fairly."

The were many things that seemed fallacious, and in no way did I have assurance about God's universal judgment, for the mere presence of hell grossly contradicted the idea of justice, and combined with the idea that the only way to avoid hell was to bow down to the creator the whole concept became too absurd to be divine. The only plausible explanation was that righteous men needed to enforce their spiritual beliefs with a threat of evil rather than a promise of heaven and thus invented the myth; citing their inspiration as divine they invoked their miserly ideals upon humanity. Anything dealing with God should focus only on love; to enter the kingdom of heaven one must strive to love, truly and generously. I was so far away.

And I asked him, "So are we're to put our faith and trust in a God who, in Numbers 15: 32-36, told Moses that a man caught gathering sticks on the Sabbath should be stoned to death. Now I know God can be see the error of his ways, as when Moses told him not to slay His people in Exodus, but He just makes too many errors, according to *The Bible*. Like when they try to leave Egypt: what he does to the Egyptians is certainly not all-loving; killing the innocent first-born. Now I love God, and there is no way I ascribe such feats to Him, only to the ignorant holy fools of the time."

The Reverend grimaced, and said, "Well, that is *Old Testament*. The *New Testament* and Jesus changes a lot of that. Most religious scholars would agree with you that parts of the *Old Testament* are incredulous."

I said, "What's incredulous is that people believe it's the word of God, and not the word of Moses or whoever rewrote *The Bible*, a human just like you or I."

"There's no use in trying to interpret *The Bible*, Paul. We will never know the precise word of God, and not all Christians believe everything in scriptures but they do believe in Jesus Christ and salvation."

"It just seems like *The Bible* complicates matters so."

"That may be true, but I think they would be complicated regardless."

"There are flashes in *The Bible* that are so pure, like in Romans, Chapter 2, for example, condemning judgment of man by men. I interpret it as meaning God will judge the man by how the man judges himself and how to live in righteousness. That seems all right, but still, the idea of judgment is difficult to come to grips with, but I see hope. Yet on the other end there are parts so muddy that it makes me think God can't be religious."

"Uh huh," he spoke slowly, "I see. As far as answers are concerned, I can't give you any. I don't think we're meant to know, for sure, just put your faith in God, and things will turn out okay."

I thought of asking him how he knew, but he would reply that he had faith. Faith and doubt do not make a good couple. It still seemed ludicrous to me, to simply say doubt ceases to exist because I put faith into God.

Reverend Martin then said, "Paul, if you pray for God and guidance, you will find what you are looking for."

I left with a handshake, thinking the talk, overall, was beneficial. It made me contemplate with greater intensity this paradox of faith. It reminded me of something Montaigne had written, 'Nothing is so firmly believed as what we least know.' For the life of me I couldn't understand why or how anyone could believe so strongly in something, especially the answer to one of the quintessential enigmas of all time; doubt had to be there. I had been praying to God for guidance, and this I continued to do.

One time, in February, I was in the living room with my mother, and I asked her, "What do you think about God?"

She was sitting on the couch. Glancing upward, she said, "Well, Paul, I believe in God."

"Yeah, but what do you think about God?"

Pausing before responding, she said, "I think it's better to believe in God than to not believe in God. It makes one's life better."

"That's all?"

She stood up and went to the piano bench, "No. Probably not, but to me God is simply there. I look out the window and see how splendid the world is, and it makes me feel God's presence."

"But our life is good, what if it weren't so good?" I said.

"We are fortunate, and we can thank God for it. But if we had poorer luck it would still be a good idea to believe, for then what else is there?"

"But it's almost like you've accepted God without really thinking about it."

She said with understanding, "No it's not. I have already spent my time wondering about God. True, now I accept God. I mean, God is love," she put her hand on my shoulder, and rubbed my back for a moment. Then she walked to the piano bench and began playing. I walked out of the room.

The following day I found my father tinkering with the family automobile, a station wagon. I asked him what he thought about God. He pulled his head out from underneath the hood, sweating, with his hair sticking to his head in matted strands, "God, hmmm. God's a pretty complex fellow. You'll have to ask a more specific question."

"Okay, then, why do you believe in God?"

"I just do."

"But don't you want to know what you believe in?"

My father said, "Man will never figure God out, we can only know parts of God. It's like the old blind men and the elephant analogy. Each blind man went up to the elephant and came back thinking the elephant was a different being, a wall, or a vine, or a tree, it's sort of like religion interpreting God in different ways. God's incomprehensible, but *The Bible* can help out. You can devote yourself to God but you have to realize you're only human and can only comprehend so much. And, let's say you do discover the truth, then what? Will you ever be sure of it, and who would believe you? I don't know what, exactly, it means when I say I believe in God, but I do know I have put my faith in a good and strong being that is just."

"Then why is the world so screwed up if there's a just God?"

"That's what heaven is for, for the worthy not to suffer."

"I see," I watched him as he stuck his head in the car.

I began to walk away, and he pulled his head back out and said, "Hey!" I turned around, and he said, "It's great that you want to learn about God. I'm sure our Reverend can find some books or something to help you. I'll talk to him next time your mother and I go to church." He smiled and watched me and my straight face, as I went back into the house.

A couple evenings later my father came into my room and placed some books on my desk, "Here, Paul, these are rather odd books. I glanced over them – yeah, they're peculiar. I'd take them with a grain of salt, if I were you. The Reverend said they're off the beaten path, but maybe you'll find something you're looking for. They're yours, as a gift."

I nodded, "All right, good deal."

My father said, "He said you'd come in to talk to him."

"I did."

"What'd he say?"

"I guess I'm not that competitive."

I asked Rob if he played ball and he told me about his career in football as a nose tackle. He was honorable mention all-league and was trying to beef up to 225 pounds from 210 so he could have a legitimate shot at making a team in college. He wanted to play at a four-year school, although he was sure he could make it at the junior college level. I listened.

He asked me what I was going to do when school was over. I told him I didn't know.

The three of them finished the champagne, and Rob and Katie started petting one another. Inevitably, the two of them said goodnight and left the room. Julie said, "You didn't drink much."

I said, "True."

Julie kissed me and we embraced on the couch, then Julie grabbed my hand, "C'mon, we can sleep in Katie's parents' room."

"Okay."

"But we have to wash the sheets tomorrow. Her parents won't be here 'til tomorrow night."

We went down a hall and into a large bedroom. A king-sized bed was in the middle of the room against the wall. Julie stood in front of me, and we put our arms around one another. She was slightly buzzed, and she purred and hummed as she started to kiss me. Soon our shoes were off and we were on the bed. She took out her braid. We undid snaps, buttons, and zippers, until we were in underpants and nothing else. I had never seen a naked woman in the flesh. The sensation of looking at her that first time filled me with awe.

I glanced at her breasts, not wanting to stare, for some reason. I wanted to kiss them but I wasn't sure if I should. But she pulled me down to her and there they were and I kissed them and each second drifted by. Whoever said time flies when you're having fun was not entirely correct. Of course, youth passes and memories seem like glimpses, but the sensations of body-warmth, fingertips slipping gently tickling down the spine, a wet tongue in the ear, a sigh, a cooing, sweat forming on the skin, were eternity. Every moment of it.

And she said, "Paul, I want you to make love to me."

I stopped and looked at her.

She said, "You can pull out."

I said, "I'm a virgin."

"That's okay, I'll help you." She started kissing me again, and stopped.

I let out, "I think I want to stay a virgin, for now."

Julie stared into my eyes, then slowly smiled, and said, "That's cool. It really is. You're different from other guys." She held me and squeezed me, "Don't think I'm a sleaze, though."

"I couldn't think that."

Then we cuddled until we fell asleep.

In the morning we woke up, affectionately, and ate breakfast by ourselves, Katie and Rob were still in bed. We said little about the previous evening, and our conversation felt different. There was more staring out into space. I drove home by myself, as Julie said she would get a ride from Katie later on. We both agreed that we had had a wonderful time, and Julie said she'd talk to me soon. I never found out whether Julie bothered to change the sheets.

I went home, and Julie didn't call all day. I went out to the bluff. Although all seemed well, I contemplated my virginity and Julie. I wasn't sure if things would be different. Julie had had a boyfriend, and probably wasn't a virgin. Naturally, I assumed this had something to do with her relation to God. She must not believe in God, I thought, and I saw the time approaching where I would have to talk to her about the subject. I'm not sure about to what extent I could have been called religious, but somehow I correlated being a virgin with godliness. Jesus was a virgin, wasn't he?

There I was with calm night, a moon behind clouds, and a humming and churning sea. And I considered the powers the mind could have if God were to guide one's decisions. I'd asked for guidance, and thus I assumed my every action was steered by divine powers. But that wasn't enough. No. My thoughts jumbled and bounced around and somehow this hypothetical notion popped up. I considered what would happen were I to receive unobstructed and definite instruction from God. All doubt would be erased, my wondering would cease and a sense of righteousness would emerge.

Yes, I look back at that night, and, luckily, I didn't fall off the bluff and tumble head over heels with my delusions to a scrambled demise of bone and flesh and rock. Instead, I left, convinced my desire to talk to God was a palpable conclusion derived from the promise in *The Bible*. God would talk to me if I wished for Him to do so.

The next day I drove along the coast for over an hour, finally stopping at a marina. I spent the day walking up and down the docks, between motorboats, yachts, cabin cruisers, sailboats, and dilapidated rowboats. I kicked the crusty rabble of dried seaweed, mussels, barnacles, and seagull leavings, into the clear water and watched them sink past schools of pogies.

When I returned that evening there was a message Julie had called. I drove to her house shortly after. From there we walked to a sandwich shop. The place was quaint, with old black and white photos of the town from the nineteenth and early twentieth centuries. We sat in a booth overlooking Front Street, and chirped about this or that for a while, and then Julie asked, "Did you have a good time at Katie's house?"

"You bet."

"I've been thinking about it a lot, you know," she paused a few seconds, and then continued, "Well, I think it's really neat you're a virgin and all. I wasn't prepared. I mean, no one's a virgin these days. But I should've guessed that you might be but I just didn't think about it. I mean, I thought about it, but I didn't. I just want you to know how I feel. I'm not a slut. I don't want you to think bad of me for wanting sex."

"I'd never think anything bad of you."

"I've only had sex with one other guy, and that was after we'd gone out a long time. I want you to know sex is meaningful to me and that you're the only guy I'd consider having sex with."

Across the table she smiled, with cute dimples, and I thought she was the one.

I said, "I only think highly of you. I want to be with you, I was just caught off guard that night. You were my first kiss, and I want you to be my first everything. You make me feel good. That night was wonderful, I'll never forget it, you're beautiful. I'd wait forever to have you."

She took hold of my hand and drew it to her mouth and kissed it, saying, "Thanks."

We went back to my car and drove to my house. Even though the wind was picking up we took the path along the top of the bluff and went into the woods, sheltered from the wind. The dark poles of trees went up around us, blue darkness outlined the tree tops, and we held and kissed each other as we stood on that floor of dirt and pine needles, with the wind whistling through the trees. I never felt so close to anyone.

In less than three weeks I had fallen completely in love. Inside my head thoughts of marriage; the gradual process of discovering sex, companionship, children, and old age; flitted in and out of my brain, but I would never contemplate these things directly. I would tell myself to be patient. In time. In a way I repressed my feelings of love, or, at least, I didn't tell Julie about them.

So my next step was to inform Julie of Christianity, and the wonderful ways of religion. Yet an incident at her house complicated matters. I was waiting in the living room of her house, as she finished a chore, and Julie's sister was flipping the channels around. She found a talk show, either it was a Christian talk show or it was a talk show about Christianity, with an attractive couple talking to an elderly gentleman who was recounting his experiences of dying and going to heaven. This old man was saying something about the tour of heaven he was given by the Angel of God when Julie's father, a husky fellow with short hair and a beard, entered the room. He ordered Julie's sister to change the channel.

Simultaneously, Julie came into the room, and she and I departed. As we were walking out the door Julie laughed and said, "Daddy doesn't like religion. He won't even let you say the C-word in our house."

"Huh?"

"Christianity."

"Christianity?"

"Yeah, to him, religion is evil. He doesn't like the concept of heaven and hell. I mean, he doesn't believe in heaven and hell, but he says if they did exist it'd sure be fairer if you went to heaven if you were a good person, and to hell if you weren't."

"What do you think?"

"I agree with him," she was leaning against my car, "We don't need religion to love. Religion takes people away from people, it makes it tougher for people to understand and accept others. Love is more important."

"Hmmm," I murmured. So there I was, not quite knowing what to do. I had never imagined there would be a problem in speaking to Julie about Christianity. I wrote in my journal:

> I have just begun to realize that having faith is a challenge. The world will cast you out all because of your belief. It makes little sense. Shouldn't we be able to believe in something and not have others tell us what to believe? I'm not sure. That is why I want to find out the truth, for if one knows the truth then shouldn't they have the right to tell others? For righteousness can only work if the righteous are right. That's why I need to know, that's why I pray for guidance ...
>
> ...Julie has presented me with a difficult problem and I pray for a solution. I think this solution may lay in the parable of the sower "The seed is the word of God." (Luke 8:11) For to plant the word in someone is like planting a seed. If I can nourish Julie, with some help from God, then it goes to follow..."

The next few days, when Julie and I spent time with one another, I was pensive. It was always on my mind, yet I was unsure about how to bring up the topic.

One Saturday afternoon Julie and I took off right after school to Hurricane Ridge, along the Olympic Peninsula. It took over an hour to reach this magnificent place, with its view of neighboring mountains and a valley. We stood over the edge of a steep decline of rocks. I was silent.

Julie asked me what was wrong and I said, "Nothing, really."

"Nothing? C'mon, tell me what's troubling you."

I prayed for a miracle, inspired by the beauty of the mountains, I breathed in, "Yeah, I guess I am troubled."

"Tell me."

"Well, it's about God."

"God?"

I turned to her, "Yeah, I'm Christian."

"You are?"

"Uh huh."

"That's quite a secret you've kept from me."

"Yup. You know, you may be the first person I've made this confession to."

She simply stared at me, so I said, "What do you think?" She

37

continued staring, and I added, "About Christianity."

And she replied, "Well, I don't think it really matters, we all live on earth together, we should try to love. That's the point of life, not to worry about god."

I kicked a pebble and watched it drop from sight, "But don't you care what happens when you die?"

"The way I see it is, if there's no god then I'll just be dead. If there is a god and he's a good god, then I'll go to heaven. And if god happens to be evil then why pray to him anyway? I shouldn't have to worry about it. Besides, there are so many people to meet, things to do, that I'd rather live for this world, not for some god."

I had come into this argument with the preconceived notion that I was right. I blurted out my speech, "It's okay that you don't believe in God. But I'm convinced He exists, and I'm convinced that if you listen to the reasons for believing in God you would be convinced as well. For you would see the light, you would see the truth, and when you see the truth you would know. One has to open one's mind to it, to God, and let the seed be planted in them."

She let go of me and stepped one foot back. In an acerbic tone she said, "I don't want you to preach to me. I really enjoy your company, don't ruin it by trying to preach. I want to share life and just be. I don't need a sermon."

"Julie," my hands made gestures as I spoke, "Don't get upset. I only want to talk to you about God because it's close to me and it's what I believe. I'm not forcing you to do anything. I'm saying God is part of me and I'd' like to tell you about Him."

Julie shook her head, "I can't believe you've been Christian all this time and haven't said anything. That's why you wanted to stay a virgin."

"Maybe it is."

"Why didn't you say anything about it?"

"I was afraid to, I thought you didn't want to hear it. And that you might react like you're reacting now. But it's an important part of me. I hope you'll accept it."

"Are you going to try and force your views on me?"

"I'll try not to."

She took a deep breath and pulled me against her. "Okay, but don't preach to me, and don't tell Daddy that you're Christian."

I kissed her on the cheek and we stood on the ridge and watched the sky and mountains below. I thought of my friend, the eagle, and how much he would enjoy this scenery, and I mentioned this thought to Julie.

My enthusiasm to tell Julie about God waned after this conversation. I didn't know whether to feel distraught or resolute, and when Julie and I were alone together we occasionally had extended periods of silence. Once, we went two days without seeing one another outside of class. Yes, I told myself, I did need a miracle.

In isolation I did think about God, I prayed, and took sanctity in this creator whose ubiquitous presence touched me. There was occasionally peace, an ephemeral moment of harmony, when I did feel my spirit immersed in love. These moments were infrequent, but they were enough to give faith to my child-like mind. And I felt justified in wishing to tell Julie of this. I was reticent in her company.

Julie became uneasy during these moments of silence. I could sense she was dismayed. I began to spend time by myself more often. I rarely called her, but I kept true to my promise of not preaching to her. Late in March she told me she wished to talk to me after school so we took a drive along the coast in my Pinto. She did the talking.

"Paul, thing's have changed."

"What do you mean?"

Julie crossed her arms as I kept my gaze, "We don't hang out together anymore. You never call me. I wonder what you're thinking all the time. What's going on? Whenever we're together you never ask me what I'm thinking or how I'm doing. You never tell me what you're thinking. You just look at the sky or the sea, and if I try to ask you something you hardly even answer."

I didn't say anything, and after a moment she asked, "Well? Don't you like me anymore?"

I answered, "Of course. I think about you a lot. You make me happy."

"Then why do you always seem so gloomy?"

"I'm just thinking."

"Then why do you always say 'nothing' whenever I ask you what you're thinking?"

"You wouldn't be interested in what I'm thinking about."

She clenched her teeth and blew out her mouth, moving her bangs slightly. Then she said, "Is it because you're thinking about God?"

I nodded my head.

"I thought so." She turned her whole body toward me so her back was nudged against the door, "Well, if you want to talk about it you can, but don't act like you're right and I'm wrong. I mean it. And I really don't care about whether God exists or if there is a monster in Loch Ness, and I know nothing can change that."

I pulled over to the side of the road, where there was a small waterfall tumbling down a rocky cliff, between trees and flowers. We got out of the car and stood watching the water erode the crevice and wet the dirt and ferns at the base of the cliff.

I said, "It's just that everywhere I go I feel a power, a goodness, and everything I read in *The Bible* confirms and explains this feeling. It's so beautiful. Don't you feel it when you look over the ocean and see the eagle fly over the whitecaps and against a cloudy sky with a sun trying to break through? Don't you feel that there's something more, that it's too beautiful not to have been created. That if there's no God then nothing makes sense. And there's a purity that grows inside me, and it feels like it is from without and from within and I feel like I am one with the universe. That is what God is to me."

Julie put her arm around me, "Paul, I do feel it. I do. But to me it's karma, or nirvana. Maybe it's God, maybe it's something else, or maybe it's just me. But it's love, and I don't care if it comes from within or without but it exists and I can just be and flow with life. My father says we should strive for self-perfection, that we should try and make ourselves better, that we should try to love and be good. He thinks religion has led us away from that even though it tries to lead us to it, and that evil's greatest victory was when religion was created because it has taken good will and turned it into pettiness. Because of religion we can't unite, except with a miracle."

40

"Don't you believe in miracles?"

"Yes."

I shook my head, "How come you're willing to listen to your father talk about God? It sounds like you've just latched onto what he said."

"Paul," she let go of me, "How can you say that without realizing that's what we all do. We're all indoctrinated with the ideas that surround us. With you it's *The Bible*, with me it's my father, but we're able to exercise our own individual will and choose what to think. If we hear something that's not our own and we think it's a good idea then how can we not be influenced?"

I said this: "But *The Bible's* the truth."

"Paul. How can you say that? I've never read *The Bible*, but I know it's not the truth."

I disagreed with her and was obstinate in believing in the Biblical portrayal of God. I said, "But what if it is true?"

"What if what's true?"

"The Bible."

"Well, if it's true that if you don't believe in God, even though you strive to love and be good, you'll go to hell. That if you can go to hell just because you didn't bow down to God, then God be damned."

"I wish you hadn't said that."

She stamped her foot. "C'mon. Be reasonable. Have you ever thought about heaven and hell and what *The Bible* says. Is that relevant in this world? It's a myth, a beautiful myth, but a myth and that's all."

"How do you know? You haven't read it."

She said nothing.

I finally spoke, "What if you saw a blind man healed by the power of God, or a cripple walk or a limb restored?"

"Then, I might believe."

"Okay, then," I folded my arms.

Julie walked a few steps away, and then returned and asked me for a hug, and as we hugged she said softly, "Paul, I care about you, you're a good guy. You're a sweetie. But you're too young to worry about God."

"But I do."

"I know you do, but we should take a day off and just forget about it. Spend time with each other. We haven't just been with each other in a long time. We could go camping this weekend- I'll tell my parents I'm staying at Katie's."

So that Saturday afternoon Julie and I went to Kalaloch, a campground and park on the coast. It was nestled in trees, on a sandy beach. Spring break had begun and although there was still a little nip in the air, it was a sunny clear day perfect for camping.

We brought a tent, two sleeping bags, firewood, hot dogs, soda pop, chips, and marshmallows. It was enjoyable, the time spent with her, and I was able to take my mind off God. We talked about how many grains of sand there were in the world, the likelihood of bears lurking in the woods, and how many marshmallows one could eat before being thoroughly nauseated by them – the number was eight. We cuddled around the fire past midnight and even the moments of silence were wonderful. We slept between the two unzipped sleeping bags, in our underwear, cozy, and it was the best time we'd had together in weeks.

The next morning, which was clear with wisps of mist dissipating quickly, we ate a breakfast of chips and marshmallows. We decided to take a hike along trails and both dressed in shorts and T-shirts, we went inland. We skipped over footbridges spread across brooks, we ran through trees and felt the morning dew sprinkle us. The sun was burning off all moisture, and before we knew it we were a couple miles in the woods. We weren't disoriented, but we were far enough away from civilization to enjoy completely our isolation.

We fell down in an embrace on green moss, not caring whether our clothing would get stained, and kissed and petted. Then Julie stood and went to a nearby branch, "Lets climb a tree, wouldn't that be fun?"

I watched as she pulled herself up to the first branch, maybe five feet from the ground, but as she settled into a sitting position she lost balance and tumbled backwards, falling on her back. Somehow the underside of her leg, behind her kneecap, got caught at the base of a small branch that had been broken and poked out from the first branch, and cut a tremendous gash into her skin. She let out a cry and I went over and saw this half-inch deep wound. It was about an inch long and was bleeding profusely. She turned over on her stomach and sobbed slowly but with force, indicative of pain.

I had no knowledge of first-aid, nor did Julie, and I wrapped up her leg in my T-shirt. She couldn't walk, and said she wanted to rest before I carried her back.

I had never thought much of channeling God's powers through me, but then, suddenly, the promises of *The Bible* and faith struck my mind. Building up my courage and nerve, pumping up my psyche, I did it. I took off my T-shirt bandage and she asked me what I was doing.

"Just let me try something."

I couldn't see the expression on her face. I pressed my hands gently on her knee over the wound, and closed my eyes, praying with everything I had for her leg to heal. For maybe a minute she was silent.

Then she said, "Paul, it's not gonna work. I don't believe in it."

"It's not for you or me to decide."

"Paul, it still hurts."

"Just wait."

But after another minute I took my hand away and saw a gash filled with coagulated blood and goo, as well as some of the sticky substance on the palms of my hands.

I said, "I guess I'm not ready,."

I felt meek.

I carried Julie back to our campsite. She was sympathetic, and didn't ridicule me. She even thanked me for carrying her and kissed me on the cheek. We found a water faucet and she washed her leg. As I packed all our things into the back of my Pinto she told me that she thought the whole thing was cute. I drove to a hospital and waited as seventeen stitches were sewn and she was wrapped and bandaged. Then I drove her home. Throughout I had the gut-wrenching feeling of failure producing questions inside.

Somehow I became more determined to strengthen my faith. I blamed myself and told myself miracles could happen; it was only the pure and chosen who were capable of performing such feats. I was a mere twerp, not worthy or ready for the power of God to be channeled through me.

Still, I wouldn't let it drop. I had concern for Julie, and felt it my duty to talk about spirituality with her. In a pious and self-righteous state I went to Julie's house. It was still spring break, two days after our camping trip. I was determined to have it out with her about God. With door open I sat in her beanbag that lay on the floor of her bedroom. I told her I wanted to talk about God.

"I thought we settled that."

I nodded, and said, anyway, "But we didn't. I thought it wouldn't matter that much, but it does. I want you to be open to what I have to say. Just listen, and let me plant the seed."

"You mean you still believe after my leg?"

"That doesn't matter, it was silly of me to think I could do it."

She sat upright on her bed, and said, "You know, Paul, I think I've been patient with you. You're in a bad mood all the time, and I'm always trying to be cheerful. I want to laugh and all I see is you and your sourpuss. We finally have a great time together, and you just want to go back to being unhappy. I care about you, but it's not the same as when we first went out. I don't want to talk about God and you know it, and if you try to I'm gonna get angry. Please respect this, Paul. Let's talk about the eagle, or mussels, or something else, but not God."

I folded my hands behind my head, "But I know that I can convince you. See it from my view, I know God exists, and I must transfer this knowledge to you."

"I don't like you telling me that you know you can convince me. Why can't you see it from my point of view?" Julie sat on her bed and crossed her arms, "I know that I don't give a damn, so what's the point?"

"What's wrong with me trying to help you? If you'd just listen to me instead of getting so angry-"

"I don't need help! You don't get it, do you?" Her vehemence caught me off guard. She went on, "You don't have a right to tell me what to think and I don't care if it is part of you. Paul, we had a great thing, don't ruin it."

"But I'm not telling you how to think."

"Yes you are." She tucked her hands underneath her legs, and said, "Maybe we shouldn't see each other for a few days, spend some time alone and think this out."

"Fine," I stood up, "I'll see you 'round."

I stormed out of the room and into the living room. Her parents looked at me, and with temerity I turned around and went straight back into her room. She was as I had left her.

"Julie, let's talk."

"No, just leave me alone. I'll call you in a couple days."

"Okay, then." I stood in her doorway for at least ten seconds, until she lifted her hand and waved goodbye. I waved back and left.

I was mad, and as I drove through town and toward my house I steamed and stewed. It wasn't fair, I thought, I was trying to help and this is what I got. I was stubborn. I parked and stomped up to my room and sat there. The possibility Julie might not be in my destiny became evident.

Yet I was hurt. I really did love Julie. All the memories of our wonderful moments returned; our first kiss, Tolo, our drives along the coast, and just a few days earlier we were cuddling in sleeping bags. The way she acted was a surprise. It began to rain, I cursed my plight, and resigned myself to saving the world on my own.

The thought that Julie would be absent from my life gave me a gnawing and painful sensation. My emptiness was growing, and something precious which I hadn't quite grasped slipped away. It had never occurred to me to cease with my talk about God. As I lay on my bed the image of myself on the spike returned, and sometimes instead of my dropping upon it, it would fall and impale me in my place. Painless and numb, I felt empty and stupid.

Paul, the Apostle, found God on the road to Damascus. He was blind and God restored his sight, he was a stranger to the spirit of God and faith came to him. Paul wrote a large portion of the *New Testament*. I imagine Paul had his doubts about the imperfect world he tread upon, but he kept his faith.

I realized that simply having faith can be its own reward. I was adamant.

Julie didn't call for two days, so I called her. It was the Friday before school was to resume. I told her I wished to speak with her and she said it'd be okay to come over. In her room I took my usual place in the beanbag and abruptly asked, "What's going on?"

"What do you mean?"

"I mean, what's going on between us?"

"Well, what do you want me to say? I want to enjoy life. I'm not on a quest for God."

"Julie, I care for you," I thought 'love', and said 'care'. "I've never cared for anyone so much."

"Are you gonna change the way you feel about God?"

"I don't think so."

"Can you accept that I'm never gonna care about God?"

I paused, and then admitted, "I don't think so."

"Well, then, I don't think we can work it out if one of us can't change. And I'm not gonna. It hurts me, and I don't want to hurt you, but maybe we're not right for each other. So maybe we should breakup."

This was unexpected, I didn't say a word. I was stunned, and finally said, "What do you mean we're not right for each other?"

Julie scooted back on the bed, "I told you, I'm never gonna be Christian. Never. I'll never care whether God exists or not. It doesn't matter. And you want to plan your life around God. Thus we can't be with one another as boyfriend-girlfriend unless one of us compromises, and I won't and you won't. Does that make things more clear?"

"Julie, don't you think we could just work this out? Give it time?"

I really didn't get it, and Julie continued, "The chemistry's gone. I've been thinking about us and how we used to have a good time together and now we don't. Paul, I like you a lot, I respect you, but you've chosen Christianity over me, and I can't deal with it. Maybe someday you'll understand and I know it sounds stupid, but maybe we can be friends when things work themselves out. I do care about you."

And so I asked her if she was sure about what she said. She was. I left.

In my room I asked myself if I'd rather have Julie or God. A concrete, flesh and blood person, or an omnipotent, vague, possibly all-loving God. And there I was, chewing on a remote piece of idealism, ready to love the idea but not being able to love.

My thoughts and writing pointed in one direction. I saw for some reason I had chosen God over Julie, part of me felt deluded, in disbelief that I had made such a decision; the other part felt pious and devoted to God. I recognized confusion and looked to a day when I would have answers, when God would talk to me.

On Saturday my father entered my room and asked me what I'd decided as far as my future was concerned. I had taken the S.A.T. and I told him that, but I added, "I don't think I'll go to school."

"You don't, huh? Then what're you going to do?" He stood by my bedroom door and leaned against the wall with his hands in his pockets.

"I'm gonna wait for God to tell me what to do."

"What?" My father rubbed his brow.

"I feel college isn't right for me, and since I don't know what is, I'll wait for God to lead me to a path."

My father frowned, "But there are Christian schools you can go to if you want to be closer to God."

"Yeah, but they probably misinterpret the actual word. I want to hear it from God, Himself."

My father reasoned, "This makes absolutely no sense. Doing nothing certainly is a wrong choice, so if you're going to make a wrong choice, why not go to school?"

I was reminded of something Socrates had said, "He is not only idle who does nothing, but he is idle who might be better employed."

I answered, "I'm not sure."

"Well, doing nothing is something. So you're all set on doing something which you're not sure about?"

College felt wrong, nothing felt right, how could I explain this, to my father, or anyone? I didn't realize I could never explain something that made no sense.

My father questioned, "What do you want in life?"

"To find God."

47

"And what are you going to do once you've found God?"

"Help the world."

My father gave a few seconds of cogitation, and said, "I admire the motive, but don't you think God would want you to help the world by doing anything, any little thing, instead of nothing? Do you think you're doing any good by sitting on your butt and waiting?"

I used this analogy: "Okay, let's say you've got a great big pile of dirt, and you need it moved. Your friend has a bulldozer, and is coming to help you. You can move the dirt all at once when he arrives. Now, would you take a shovel and try to move the dirt yourself if you knew your friend was coming over with a bulldozer?"

My father grimaced, and said, "So, you're waiting for the great big bulldozer in the sky to come and assist you in helping mankind?"

"If you want to look at it that way."

What could my father say to this? What would anyone say? He stared at me, "You're crazy. You really are. I love you, and your mother and I will always support you, but you're crazy. I don't know how it came about," he put his hands on his hips, "But it did. At least your motives are good. I'll tell you what; there'll come a time when you'll have to choose between college and living on your own, just remember, we aren't going to support you for too long after school. Okay?"

"Fine with me."

"Okay, then," and my father left my room. He immediately returned, and asked me, "Why don't you go to church and talk to a preacher?"

"I want to get instruction from God."

My father shook his head slowly as he walked out of my room for the second time.

Spring break ended and school resumed. I talked little with Julie. If we ran into each other we would acknowledge one another's presence with a glance, little else. Dennis asked me what was up, and I told him Julie and I were no longer seeing each other. Dennis said, "I figured that, I saw her holding hands with Terry at a party last weekend."

"Only that faith is all one needs."

"That's it?"

"Pretty much."

My father sat in a chair by my desk and said, "I'm almost fifty years old, and I've wondered the same things as you. Most people have. Is there a God? Is he fair? Eventually everyone discovers the same thing, whether or not they fly around the world and climb every mountain and sail every sea, they discover that they only know what they know, and that they must make the best of it."

"Then that's what I'll do."

He stood and walked to the door, "No doubt about that."

When he left I looked at the books. One was about Armageddon and The Tribulation. Another was titled *The Pyramids: Proof of God*. And next to it was a book called *The God of Rock*, and it appeared to be about the evils of rock music. The last one focused on demons and demon possession.

I spent the next few days looking them over. They fascinated me the way fairy tales and myths do. The book on rock music presented the evil themes of rock: Drugs, Rebellion, Sex, Satanism, and False Religions. There was a chapter explaining how Satan was Lord of the Airwaves, and thus he controlled radio. Now this seemed absurd, and, if anything, it made me curious to listen to rock music. The meat of the book went over specific groups. I'd only heard of some; The Beatles, Led Zeppelin, Pink Floyd, The Doors; and it explained how they were spreading the devil's propaganda. I knew little about these groups, but I had heard 'Yesterday' and 'Hey Jude' by The Beatles, and I couldn't imagine that they were songs of evil.

The book on pyramids introduced some information about these great structures. The pyramid was an architectural and engineering phenomenon, its dimensions were lined up to perfection, mathematically, astronomically, and geographically. The Great Pyramid, the book explained, was without religious graffiti, while all other lesser pyramids were covered inside and out with the scrawls and drawings done by the Egyptians, who worshipped everything. It seemed very unnatural that the Great Pyramid would be devoid of these religious scribblings.

Underneath the Great Pyramid was a time line, which charted historical events with accuracy, and it indicated that humanity's time was over at around the year 2000; this seemed a bit fantastic. The material needed to build the pyramid, and the manpower to bring the materials to its present location and construct the pyramid were simply too huge for it to have been made without divine intervention. Of course, I was skeptical.

Which led me to the book about Armageddon. It used ambiguous quotes from Revelations, ones which mentioned the "ten-headed beast," the number "666," the seals, and creatures that were any combination of dragon, lion, eagle, bear, or whatever. It touched upon some of the prophets, such as Daniel and Solomon, and their visions; and with vague quotes and abstract facts it constructed solid proof that, yes, indeed, the apocalypse was approaching within our lifetime, probably in the next ten years. It quoted Revelations fiercely.

Revelations, this book of angels and devils and serpents, God and Magog, the Alpha and Omega, its phantasmagorial carnival of creatures and the violence of nature, God's wrath, salvation, judgment day, and the myriad of prophecies, left me boggled. Of all books in *The Bible*, Revelations is the most cryptic. The nature of it was foreign to me, and, although I couldn't decipher the meaning of the book, I put little faith in anyone being able to translate those illusory visions into proof that the world was headed for holy destruction. Who was more bewildered, myself or the author of that strange book trying to explain the meaning of Revelations? Yet there was a part of me that considered the possibility that perhaps religious turmoil, a battle between good and evil, was approaching, and I could have a role to play in it. The fact that I entertained this notion, although only with a sliver of seriousness, questions my reasoning ability.

The next book was about demon possession. The author had died and been led around heaven and earth by angels before being returned to life in this world. He'd seen how demons worked in influencing human's lives when he had his brief meeting with the afterworld. He had seen separate demons, each with its own title for its own iniquity. There were demons of Greed, Hate, Power, Lust, Covetousness, Sloth, Perversity, Selfishness; as well, there was a hierarchy within the network of demons, likewise, with angels. It was strange, this theory of spiritual forces at work, and the idea of a battle in one's own mind between good and evil. For example, a demon of Lust would tell the individual to have sex and he or she would act upon this if the individual lacked a bond with an angel. The only way to rid oneself of demonic influences was through prayer and faith. Now I thought the book had an interesting point of view, but, overall, it was ridiculous beyond comprehension. I thought people should put faith in love and God, not absurdity and pure myth.

I wasn't going to bother trying to interpret the misinterpretations of God. Being a sheep is an inane way to devote oneself to God. There were problems with religion, and the world needed someone to clarify the meaning of God so people could unite. Religious strife, such as in the Middle East and Northern Ireland, was difficult to fathom. I thought, maybe my purpose was to erase the ties people have with religion and bring them closer to God, and love. And, I thought, it was possible to do this.

By the beginning of spring I was getting restless. I had spent a winter in solitude, writing, reading, playing the piano, and I felt a twinge of impatience. The long nights of watching the ocean change from serene deep blue to raging black to calm again were becoming tiresome. I was ready for the future.

At least it was spring, and I could appreciate nature. There were also moments of quiet contemplation out on the bluff or the dock where I did feel satisfied and content to wait. God knew I would have to pack up and go soon, and I was sure He would push me on my way.

My father came to me one afternoon as I stood in our backyard. He asked me, "All right, Paul, so, have you come up with anything in your wait for God?"

"I'm still waiting, but I can feel it's gonna be soon, any moment, I'm sure of it."

"Mmmmm," he held his hands on his waist. He said, "Well, if God doesn't talk to you," he couldn't help curling his lips a little, "You can go to school. The money is still there for you. Your year's almost up,"

There was a long period of silence where we looked around,

at the dirt, up in the trees or sky, and then I said, "Fair enough."

Seemingly satisfied, my father stepped away.

One evening in May, as the sun set, I was playing the piano in the living room. On the lacquered, dark wood surface of the piano streaks of scarlet and dark blue were reflected, I was feeling peaceful. I heard my father enter the room, I stopped playing, and all I heard were jaw movements. He was watching me, perhaps he wished to talk. But I resumed playing, and in a short while I heard his soft steps leave the room.

That night I dreamt I saw his face, with dried tears on his cheeks, for he had been weeping. It seemed silly, in a way, because I don't ever remember him crying, but it made me think of how we never communicated. All I had to do was approach him, and say "I love you." That would be enough. But I didn't, and I don't know why. I do know that I never confronted my emotions. And what about guidance? Where were you, God?

I remember that day. It was June 29. I had spent the day talking to the madrona trees, and in the evening I walked through town and wondered about Julie. Was she still in California? Would I ever see her again? She deceived me, yet I didn't hold it against her. It made her human. I came home and played the piano, the moon was out and my mother was asleep. My father was on a business trip in Tacoma and wasn't expected until after midnight. It got late and I felt drowsy and went upstairs to bed.

My mother woke me up, it must have been around two a.m. Her face was doleful, with a twinge of panic, and she said, "Come with me Paul, your father's been in an accident."

I was tired but as this seeped into me, all drowsiness left. I put on my clothes and we drove to the hospital at the University of Washington. My mother told me that the car that hit him was driven by a drunk man, who had died instantly. The driver evidently had a warrant out on him and was trying to escape from the police. My father was driving his car, and although he was wearing a seatbelt, it lacked a shoulder strap. His head smashed into the dashboard and his skull was fractured. He was in a coma. They had flown him by helicopter to Seattle.

We drove in the station wagon. It seemed motionless. My mother stared straight ahead and didn't say a word. The whole ride I prayed, repitiously, "Don't let him die, God. All I ask is that you let him live. I'd rather suffer than see him die and my mother alone. I will suffer if he dies and my mother is alone. Let me take the burden. God, please, you have the power, let him live so I can tell him I love him. Don't let me drift downriver without a paddle. Let me earn love, Yours and his, just don't let him die."

When we reached the hospital nurses in white led us around. A doctor told us the news: when my father arrived he was brain dead, and by the time we had made it he had already been pronounced dead.

I was too cold to touch, with skin of steel. My father was dead, and there was the spike. Piercing me.

Part II

"Just because you're writing a novel about your own madness ...
...you have suddenly become a literary critic

well, then, tell me,
of all these writers ... whose pain is real?
what? yes, I might have guessed - your pain is real."
                                        —Charles Bukowski

It took the first eighteen years of my life to discover that, maybe, there was meaning in religion, and the subsequent devotion following. This period of devotion lasted for less than two years. My apostasy took hours. I wrote:

Somewhere in the Book of Truth there should read: Ask and ye shall be pissed upon. Seek, and ye shall fall into a pit of black excrement laced with tape worms. Knock, and either silence shall greet you, or, if the door is opened a putrescent mist shall envelope you, never for you to be released until you are a withered scab; left to dissipate in the wind. For he that asketh is deceived ...

...So this is what I was destined for? Was I deceived by God? Why blame imagination? Did *The Bible* deceive me? No, I deceived myself. This existence of God, it is like the existence of planes, lines, and points. It is a

69

mere idea lacking concrete actuality, and it is necessary for things to be explained to the satisfaction of those who aren't interested in the truth. As if things needed to be explained. Is this what I was destined for? Well, fuck destiny...

I had lived entirely for myself, chasing a phantasm; no more.

After the funeral my mother and I drumbled about the house in cadaverous rhythm. To see her so disconsolate was awful. All along I'd been concerned about not being able to communicate with my father when here was this woman, my mother, whose existence I had taken for granted. This saturnine lady and I her son, were tied together.

I asked my mother, "Did you pray?"

"What?

I asked again, "Did you pray that he'd live?"

We were in our living room, the window was cracked open for the night air to cool us. My mother sat on the couch and I was standing near the window. Calmly she spoke, "Of course, I prayed and prayed." She hardly moved her lips, "I prayed so much. "

I said, "Your prayers weren't answered. Aren't you mad? Don't you feel cheated? Betrayed?"

My mother looked at me, "I never expected God to save your father. I just hoped and prayed because it made me feel better. It was all I could do. It's not right to expect God to answer your prayers."

"What do you mean it's not right? Then it's not right for *The Bible* to tell you to pray and that your prayers shall be answered. You might as well sacrifice a small, furry, dumb animal if it makes you feel better. You pray and then you die. What does it take for people to discover the two have nothing to do with each other?"

"Paul-"

"I loved him. And I prayed. Hard. I didn't want him to die."

"Paul, would you be feeling better right now if you hadn't prayed?"

One tear trickled down my eye, but it was enough to make my head gently throb, and I said, "I love you."

She smiled, ever so slightly, and I could barely hear her say,

"I love you, Paul."

I walked outside.

There they were; the stars, the moon, the gentle hum of the sea and the paper cut-outs of the trees against the night; there they were.

The summer passed slowly through translucent eyes that tried to see the blue sky and the cotton clouds and the eagle in flight and the silver shards of light dancing upon the ocean. In a continual state of lament, I wanted to break down and weep, but I could never cross the line and cry. I tried to, but all I could do was stand outside and exist.

One day I went to Julie's house. Her mother told me that Julie wouldn't be back until Christmas break, but she'd pass the word to Julie that I'd stopped by. I said thanks. Then, having heard of my father's death, she offered me her condolences. I thanked her again.

I wrote infrequently, and played the piano often. Time simultaneously accelerated and decelerated, it passed slowly but when it was over it seemed like it hadn't existed. Whenever I tried to read or concentrate for an extended period of time I became mentally fatigued or plain apathetic.

In late August I found my mother as she sat at our dining room table preparing to eat, and I asked her if there was still money saved in my college fund. She nodded her head, "With life insurance and the money we've saved, you'll be able to go anywhere you wish."

But I had no particular desire to be anywhere else. I simply didn't want to be there, at home. I needed a change of scenery, a place where I wouldn't dwell on the past. A question surfaced in my mind, right then, and I asked, "Mom?"

She raised her head.

"Why'd you raise me the way you did?"

Swallowing a mouthful of salad, she said, "We wanted you to have everything, including freedom to choose how you wanted to live. We gave you your individuality. You got what you needed, but as you were maturing we noticed a gap. You became distant, caught up with yourself, and we were distant in return. We felt that with time you would mature and wish to know about us, but it never happened."

"It never did," I agreed.

"Your father had a quote to justify the way we raised you. It was by Joubert - 'Children have more need of models than of critics.'"

I nodded, then asked, "What'd you think of me?"

She thought for a bit, and then said, "Your father thought you were on your way to doing something, but you needed to mature and lose your high ideals and some of your pride. But he felt in time things would come together."

"Come together," I murmured. I bit my lip, "I never talked to you, I don't know why. My reason may have been that I saw no reason to."

"That's true. It's funny, we didn't think you talked to anyone. When ,you started seeing Julie we were surprised. Your father and I were so busy with each other, and so sure that you would grow just by being around books and beauty, that we never gave you enough love. But you were always on our minds." She slid her arms on the table and set her fork down, "You missed out on a normal childhood. I don't know how you thought you could actually talk to God, and when I heard that was your goal I wasn't sure how to feel. Instead of trying to talk to you about it, your father and I waited for you to figure it out on your own. I sometimes think we did nothing to raise you except run a hotel and give you free rent. I've never been able to communicate well, your father was the one exception, which is one of the reasons why I loved him so much."

She looked at me.

I had nothing more to say, for the time being.

However, that night I thought about her. Was it important to communicate? I'd told her I loved her, she knew that, and she said she loved me. I knew that. Did I need to tell her about my relation with Julie, or how I hurt about my father's death, or how I felt betrayed by God, or, more realistically, betrayed by myself? To walk in that house without my father around to ask me how the madrona trees were doing, or to tell me I was crazy; it was a void never imagined.

The next day my mother gave me some college pamphlets

that had been saved during my senior year by my father. He had taken the trouble to collect them and never bothered to show me. I looked over all the universities and realized it was too late to register at anyplace except at a community college. I sat at my desk in my room and flipped brochures over, occasionally glancing out the window, and real sorrow entered my life. Finally, I decided upon a college in Seattle, and planned on driving there to find an apartment and register for school.

All the while the gut feeling remained, I needed vindication. I hadn't answered anything or found out anything, and now I backtracked to the fork in the road where I had chosen God and asceticism. I was ready to take the other path .

One evening I came home, and to my surprise I was greeted in the living room by my mother in front of a television set.

I asked, "Why didn't you tell me you were gonna buy a TV?"

My mother answered, "I didn't think you'd care."

I said nothing.

"There are some good things on sometimes, and it relieves my boredom."

"Uh huh."

She had started going to church regularly, and every Wednesday night met with a group of ladies from church. Once they were over when it was mother's turn to be host. It was strange to have a house filled with about seven or eight ladies. I left them to their activities. Also, my mother continued to play the piano and she kept the house running.

I tried to watch television, but it irritated me with its frequent commercials, annoying canned laughter, and plastic life. My father was right, it was garbage and junk. Yet since it filled my mother's spare time I said nothing.

As September rolled around the shock of my father's death began to wear off. I started writing more frequently. I took a trip to Seattle and registered at Seattle Central, a community college on Capitol Hill. The city intrigued me. It was so different. People ambling about on streets and sidewalks, underneath tall buildings. Also, I secured a studio.

I had a few days home before my departure to school. It felt good to be finally leaving. Although, in a way I felt sad to leave the piano, the house, the scenery, the town, and my mother. Yet, when my last day finally approached, I was relieved to be gone.

I loaded my belongings into the Pinto. My mother followed me in her small station wagon with the rest of my stuff, and we went to Seattle. The task of moving into my studio was strenuous, and when I was finished I hugged my mother and kissed her on the cheek. She left. I wondered what was in store for her the rest of her life.

Capitol Hill was a depressing area, it looked so ominous that I gladly paid an extra forty dollars a month to park my car in the garage beneath the apartment building. The garage was a dungeon with a laundry room in its corner. My studio was on the third floor of this brick building on Bellevue, between Pike and Pine Streets. The studio had a hard wood floor, and its dimensions were about thirty feet by fifty. Near the door was an entrance to a bathroom which had a tub, shower, and a murky white porcelain sink and toilet. My window was on the side of the building, and I had a not very splendid view of the dirty, yellow brick wall of another apartment building, with shades drawn on all the windows. Just above this building I could see the skyline of Seattle. There was a grocery store a half block away.

It didn't take long for me to figure out that I would become stir crazy in that apartment if I didn't find something to do. I had furnished the place with a desk by the window, a table, a bed, two straight chairs, one easy chair, and a bookcase. The room, with its cream colored wall paper, was dull and I could only read and write for so long. A piano would have been nice.

When I went outside the apartment I saw filth. My first close-up glimpse of the city showed me concrete, asphalt, and brick, all of it dirty. Everywhere broken bottles, cigarette butts, torn papers, cardboard boxes, splotches of tar, and all sorts of garbage surrounded the poor characters who infested the allies and streets. This presence of squalid rabble was disturbing. Sometimes I would walk by bums squatting on the pavement asking for spare change. A few looked over forty years of age, even fifty or sixty, although they had probably aged rapidly. I was asked for bus fare, a quarter, or a smoke. I had no experience with the drug culture, but I assumed that drugs and alcohol played a lead role in this hive. People either ignored me, scowled at me, or their eyes would plead.

I wasn't eager to explore my neighborhood, nor did I want to drive around the city, for I was still uncomfortable in traffic. The city made me feel so small. Nature always humbled me, and although I felt tiny as I would stand on the bluff, I would have a sense of continuity and belonging. I had no immediate desire to be part of the city.

The Sunday evening before school I made myself drive into the city, because I was bored. I looked upon all sorts of people in the night light: well-dressed, the working class, people spending a night out, and those whose home was literally the city. Each person had a separate life and struggle. They seemed wretched, abject; the rich and poor, and I thought of the masses of people, for this was only one city. In a way it was frightening. I saw that the number of people is simply too great to hope that everyone can be touched, and for every one person I encountered there was a million or more I would never affect, and would never affect me. To think I had imagined I could do something for humanity. I felt puny.

I returned to my studio. I had brought all my books from home to fill the bookcase. On my desk was a typewriter, dictionary, thesaurus, and my journal. Yes, this studio was dull, but I cared little, it was shelter, and my own little world. It would suffice.

Seattle Central was only a few blocks away, and I walked in the gray morning mist to my first class. It was strange being in a classroom with such a mix of people. There were middle-aged people, people from different ethnic groups; the class was more diverse than any I'd encountered. In front of me and to my left sat a girl with a nose ring, she was pretty, but I had never seen anyone up close with a nose ring, Her hair was long, and it had evidently been dyed red. She seemed preoccupied and didn't look around much, and was wearing a black leather jacket, black jeans, necklaces, earrings, a metal chain around her waist, and black boots. From the side I could see, on the flap of her right nostril, a ring. I tried to get a better glimpse by leaning forward, and I saw this thin, curved piece of golden metal embedded in the flap of her nose. It resembled a wart hog's tusk. The girl was strikingly pretty other than that, but I wasn't thrilled by the nose ring.

I was wearing jeans and a light blue T-shirt, along with my army jacket. I had let my hair grow a little after my father's death, but it was only about halfway past my ears on the side, and almost reached my shoulders in the back. I could see how, in certain crowds, dressing normal could be considered peculiar.

The teacher explained the syllabus. I hadn't bought any books. We were to read a few short stories, a play by Shakespeare and a novel by Dickens. The teacher went over his grading procedure, and we were dismissed. My other two classes followed the same format, an explanation and introduction to the upcoming quarter.

I went to the student bookstore and bought the necessary books. I decided to find a place to eat on Broadway, the main strip of Capitol Hill. I ended up at a pizzeria that sold slices. As I waited to order, the girl with the nose-ring entered and stood next to me. She swayed a little, as if she were dancing to a tune inside her head, but she wasn't wearing a walkman. As I turned to look at her she said, "You're in my English class, aren't you?"

"Yeah."

I looked at her straight on, she seemed to struggle for something to say, "You gonna have some pizza?"

"Eventually," I glanced at the girl behind the counter who hadn't taken my order.

The girl with the nose-ring said, "They have really great pizza here." Her voice didn't quite fit her appearance. It was cute and dainty, and while she was slender, slightly taller than average, and cat-like, her black and silver garb contradicted her delicate tone.

I was asked for my order, and I gave it and received a soda and a couple slices. I walked away, and the girl with the nose ring said, "Well, goodbye."

I turned and said, "If you want, after you've gotten your meal you can join me."

She stared at me, and I couldn't tell if she had heard or not. I sat down and started eating, and soon afterwards she came to my table for two, and sat across from me. I asked her, "If you think the pizza's so great, then why didn't you get any?"

"I didn't feel like any."

We made direct eye contact. She had very pretty, blue-green eyes.

As I ate I agreed, it was good pizza. She sat across from me, drinking from her glass and not saying a word, so I finally asked her, "What's your name?"

"Bridgette."

"That's a neat name. Bridgette what?"

"Bridgette Cole," her hand fidgeted in front of her, as if she didn't know whether to itch herself or take a sip of soda.

I was interested in her. I didn't know what to say and my curiosity couldn't resist, "Why do you wear that nose-ring?"

She blushed and stammered, "I don't like the real world," she paused, "So if I wear a nose ring I'm not part of it."

Okay. I gave her my puzzled expression, with lips pursed and eyebrows wrinkled, and said, "I think you just want to be different, which is what everyone wants. Thus, by trying to be different you are actually proving to be the same as everyone else."

"Oh," her voice squirmed and she pushed herself away from the table, "So you don't like my nose-ring?" She placed her hand by her mouth and gnawed slightly on a painted nail. Everything about her was slender, fragile; her arms, the bone structure which accented her cheeks, even her pretty eyes were delicate.

"What?"

"I mean, if there's something wrong with me then why did you ask me to sit with you?"

"Listen," I leaned back in my chair and crossed my arms, "You wear a nose-ring, you should expect some shit. I don't want to offend you, but I had to ask. I've had a sheltered life, I've never seen what the natives do in the city."

"Well, okay," she stood up, "I've gotta go now."

"Yeeesh, Bridgette, I'm sorry-" but she was walking away. I wondered if she would attend class the next day.

She did. She came into class a couple minutes late and sat three desks in front of me. I tried to make eye contact with her to no avail. After class I followed her into the hall, and from behind I tapped her shoulder, she turned around and I said, "Hey, I'm really sorry about yesterday. What I said wasn't nice."

She stared at me.

I added, "It was rude. I didn't think you'd get upset but you did, and I apologize."

She kept staring, and for a few seconds I thought she was going to walk off, but instead she said, "Okay. Thanks."

"It's all right, then?"

"Sure."

"By the way, my name's Paul," I held out my hand and she shook it by barely grasping hold of it for what couldn't have been a second. I said, "Would you like to join me for lunch somewhere this afternoon?"

She shrugged, "Sure, but where?"

"You know the area."

She said, "There's a 7-11 at Broadway and East Harrison. You know where it is?"

"No, but I can find it."

"Okay, meet me there at say, 1:30."

"Great, I will." We parted. I was surprised at myself. My asking her out wasn't premeditated.

When I reached the 7-11 she was there waiting. I asked her if she had any special place in mind. She led us to a deli. As we walked I said, "You know, I've never littered. In the place where I grew up if I saw litter I'd burn a little. But here, in the city, this trash doesn't bother me as much. It's almost as if it belongs in the city."

"You don't like the city?" she asked.

"I'm not familiar with the city. Let's just say it's not love at first sight."

She said, "I've lived in Seattle all my life. You get used to it, the noise, the crowd. It's all part of something else, not you. You learn to ignore it."

We reached this small sandwich shop. Inside we ordered. I was stunned at how pretty she was. She had a smooth complexion. Her features were not quite perfect, her high cheekbones and tiny nose were made of porcelain. Her eyes were placed

78

perfectly in her head, with a sorrowful, blue-green luster. She was truly beautiful, and the nose-ring seemed such an absurd addition. It distracted me as we talked. This time, I tried to be tactful.

"Bridgette, I know you don't like me to say anything about it, but I'm interested in why you're wearing a nose-ring. I've never known anyone with one. To me it's odd. Now I think you're a beautiful person, even wearing it, but it's, I don't know, it says something and I don't think I hear it."

She sighed, "Paul, it's just something I like to do. I like the look, I like how other people look with one. I think you'd look all right with long hair and an earring, but I don't wonder why you don't have longer hair or an earring."

"Okay, that's fair enough," I wouldn't ask her about the nose-ring anymore. I planned on letting my hair grow, but I wasn't about to wear an earring. Even on girls I had never seen the point of wearing them.

The deli walls were filled with posters and advertisements; for openings of art galleries, musical events, theater, an arts and crafts fair, a film festival, and so on. There were plants, and a fan kept the room cool. The building was old with a pleasant, musty smell.

I asked her a question about the city, "It seems like you can never be completely private in the city. Don't you ever want to be alone?"

She set her elbows on the table, "I'm lonely sometimes."

"I mean, don't you ever want to stand on top of a bluff and scream with no one to hear you except birds, squirrels and rabbits, and nature? Don't you want to get away?"

"Sort of, but you can in the city, once you know what it's about." Her lips were perfect. They were scarlet, yet I couldn't tell if she wore lipstick. She asked, "If you don't like the city then why are you here?"

This was a good question. I took a bite of my sandwich and contemplated over the taste of corned beef and Swiss cheese, "I've been sheltered all my life. I've decided that I would come to the city to taste and see and smell as much of the sweet and as much of the putrid as I can. Maybe I'll find out something about life, or people, or myself. Or, maybe, I'll get fed up, go somewhere else, more lost than ever."

Our eyes were now locked, and she asked, "Are you a poet?"

I had read good poetry and never considered myself a true poet. Where would humanity be if bad poetry ceased to be admired?

But I said, "I guess."

She asked me where I was from and I told her. She'd never heard of it, so I described it for her; the bluff, the beach, the ocean, the eagle, the dock, and the town. "I will end up in a place like that, it's the only type of atmosphere where I can have peace of mind." I said this even though I had never had peace of mind in my life. We left the deli and walked on Broadway.

She lived a little off Broadway, and I accompanied her home. Her apartment was on the bottom floor of a building. Thanking me for taking her there, she asked for my phone number. I told her I didn't have a phone.

"No phone?"

"I just moved in."

"Well, then, we'll see each other in class?"

"I guess," my foot tapped against the sidewalk, in front of her door. "Maybe Friday we could do something."

"Yeah, okay," she said.

We said our good-byes, and I left, thinking she might be the only woman in the world who could look attractive with a nose-ring.

That evening I considered my appearance in the eyes of other people. If I had any concern for this in the past it had been minimal, but in the city most everyone, almost by necessity, was vain. For the most part I had thought I never gave a damn what others looked like, but I realized everyone I saw in the city I judged solely on appearance. As for what others thought of me, I didn't think I'd care, but I'd never known anyone whose thoughts about my appearance overly concerned me. Not my parents, peers, or teachers. Julie, maybe, but I couldn't remember it. I was more vain intellectually than physically, and always equated my being a loner with a life of wisdom, looking down on those who participated in daily badinage as trivial. Maybe I was wrong. There's a chance isolation could be related to close-mindedness. When my only company was myself I would make judgments about people whom I knew little about. I saw myself as narrow-minded, realizing every time I made a judgment I should turn it inward.

In my room I saw how extraordinary the city could be at night. The lights and skyline and colors and glow of orange, red, blue, green, yellow, and white filtered through architecture. It wasn't bad for man-made scenery.

Bridgette didn't appear in class on Wednesday or Thursday, but she came on Friday. I asked her where she'd been and she told me she hadn't felt like attending class. She hadn't forgotten our plans for the evening, and gave me her phone number. I called her from a phone booth later in the day, and we made plans to meet on Broadway. When we met she was wearing her leather and metal, and carrying a black purse. As we walked we passed bums, the young, the elderly, the rebels and toughs, the dope pushers, people scurrying about to meet appointments, and others preparing for the weekend. For a couple blocks we walked without saying anything. I noticed the reactions of people as we approached them. Some men gave Bridgette a hard, long look. Most people ignored us, one scraggly fellow asked us if we wanted any 'smoke.'

As Bridgette and I walked I sensed that we shared something. I figured we both had a mutual pain or longing that brought us together. We must have gone four blocks when I asked, "Where are we going?"

"To a friend's, we're almost there."

Soon, we took a turn at a street and went down a block and a half, then we turned at an alley. There was a three-story weather beaten house, tall, large and white, the paint was beginning to chip, with stairs on the outside, which we climbed. On the second floor we stopped at a small porch and Bridgette knocked at the door.

A tall, skinny guy with black, curly hair surrounding his head answered, "Bridgette!" They hugged, and Bridgette introduced him to me. His name was Nathan.

We shook hands. Then we went through a kitchen and into a

living room. Two guys sat on a couch, and two girls were sitting on the floor, leaning against a wall. I was introduced to everyone, and I took a seat in a chair in the corner of the room, by the couch. Bridgette stayed in the kitchen and talked with Nathan. I was pretty sure I was the only one in the apartment that didn't have an earring. Everyone wore at least one, except Nathan, and he might have but I wasn't able to see his ears. I also stood out in that I wasn't wearing black, and instead of boots I wore sneakers. The walls were filled with posters and prints of rock groups and art, a stereo was stacked against the wall, next to a cabinet filled with compact discs, tapes, and records. There was a coffee table in the middle of the room, and upon it were candles and a bong. On the wall behind the couch was a Grateful Dead poster, and on both sides of the couch were plants.

Sitting on the coffee table between the couch and my chair was a book on Salvador Dali. I looked through it and found some intense pictures of paintings, but on the back there was a quote by Dali:

The fact that I, myself, at the moment of painting, do not understand my own painting, does not mean that these pictures have no meaning; on the contrary, their meaning is so profound, complex, coherent, and involuntary that it escapes the most simple analysis of logical intuition.

This was in big, black letters, as if the editor or authors of the book thought this was very impressive. I couldn't tell who was the bigger idiot, these editors, or Dali. I didn't like the way Dali took his work so seriously. It was pompous and asinine. Who did this lunatic think he was? To think that this fool thought he had a meaning, a meaning that was relevant. He said nothing to me. A thought struck me. Who was I to accuse others of self-centeredness? It is an odd feeling to see oneself as a hypocrite.

The two guys on the couch were having a discussion. Todd, furthest from me, said, "You gotta respect Steven King, he's a master, he truly is."

The other, Perry, countered, "No I don't. He wastes his talent on tripe. If he's a genius why doesn't he get a grip and write something that says something. He could create art, not just silly horror stories."

"But they're not just silly horror stories," Todd said, "He can write some pretty in-depth stuff. You ever read any of his stuff?"

"Nope."

Todd gave a hesitant glance, moving his hands behind his head as if he were going to throw something but changed his mind at the last moment, he said, "You probably don't like Clive Barker, either."

Perry shook his head.

Todd continued, "He writes horror, but he's really cool. He says something which I think is a really bold statement. He says that evil exists, and that people are evil just because they like to be. Steven King thinks evil has a cause, like a child becomes evil because he is influenced by a neighbor who used to torture people for the Nazis. But Barker's more honest about it. He knows that people are evil because they enjoy it." Everytime Todd said the word "evil" he made a gesture with his hand.

"Evil exists," Perry glanced at me as I listened, "But I don't need to read horror to be enlightened about it."

"But don't you think it's a pretty bold statement to write about evil the way it is?" Todd said.

"Gee, that's pretty bold," Perry said.

I didn't see Todd's point. Surely some people enjoyed doing wrong, and others felt guilt when they did wrong and tried to stop doing wrong, and others did wrong because they were influenced by evil. I thought evil should be described as honestly and completely as possible, for then the reader could see evil as it was and then make his or her own judgments upon it, assuming one could look at evil objectively. A part of me may have been fascinated by evil, but I certainly didn't find it entertaining. King and Barker, it seemed, thought evil should be made into amusement; playing upon what fascinates mankind. But they were successful, so what could I say?

Perry responded to Todd, "There are some pretty good novels out there that take a serious look at the battle between good and evil in human nature, and these novels aren't just fantasy pieces of shit. I'm never gonna read Clive Barker or Steven King, I'm completely convinced they have nothing important or relevant to say."

Todd shook his head, "How can you say that when you've

never read anything by either of them?"

"Hey, if I had the time to read everything, I would, but when I can choose between intelligent writers who give a shit about real life or Steven King, I know what I'm gonna choose. I'm certainly not gonna waste my time on a second-rate writer."

Todd held up his hand, "He's a rich, second-rate writer."

Perry shook his head and looked at me, "What do you think?"

I said, "I haven't even seen a Steven King movie, but I'm not too interested in horror."

Bridgette and Nathan then entered the room. Bridgette did a twirl in the center of the room and ended up sitting on the rug in front of my chair. Nathan went to a drawer and pulled out a bag of what I assumed was pot. He loaded the bong and gave it to Bridgette, along with a lighter. She took a hit. The bong went to the two other girls, and around the room.

Perry offered, "Take a hit?"

"Sure." I received the paraphernalia, and lit the herb in the bowl.

Perry told me, "Put your finger over the carb." He pointed to a small hole in the side of the cylinder. I followed his directions, and relit the pot. I sucked smoke inside until my chest popped, and then I quickly set the bong on the floor. I was coughing badly.

Perry laughed, "You haven't smoked much ganja in your life, have you?"

Perry had long, blonde hair that went about halfway down his back. He was slim, tall, and wore a leather jacket, ripped jeans, and reptile skin boots.

I replied, "Nope."

The bong was passed around a few times, and I took a hit everytime it was my turn. I soon felt like a C-clamp was stuck to my head and my thought was in the center. There was an M. C. Escher drawing on the wall, and I followed those steps for the longest time as they spiraled and criss-crossed in contradictory geometry.

Nathan played compact discs, and when we were all high he replaced the fast-paced grunge with a mellow acoustic sound. I enjoyed listening to music and sitting in the room, relaxing.

84

And as I sat there I knew I desired to lose my virginity. I wanted Bridgette to scrape my back with her painted nails, and I wanted to experience myself enmeshed in scarlet flesh. That loony religious demon book popped into my mind, and I reiterated its presumptions; but no pitchforked devil was coaxing me on to copulation, it was myself wishing to act upon natural sexual instinct. And if I enjoyed doing it I would repeat the act if possible. The witch doctor that invented the demon theory was living in a fabricated world.

So I sat, baked, in that room. Bridgette sat nearby but said little, no one did, we were stoned. By two a.m. I was tired, everyone in the room seemed to be, as well. I asked Bridgette if she wanted to go, she did, and I pulled her to her feet. I thanked Nathan, Bridgette gave him a hug, we said goodbye to everyone, and left.

We went outside, down the stairs, and into the alley. As we walked to my apartment we held hands. I said, "You know, Bridgette, that was my first time stoned. I mean, really, and you know what? It wasn't too bad. I enjoyed it. No shit. Hmmm. Believe it or not, one year ago I never would've guessed I'd ever smoke pot. I thought drugs were evil. But tonight was very peaceful. It sorta says something about the ignorance of this country, when we risked going to jail tonight by smoking pot, and people can drink legally in bars. That's pretty fucking dumb, isn't it?"

Bridgette said, "Uh huh."

I said, "Pot's much better than alcohol, I can't understand it. I mean, alcohol seemed a lot more powerful. I was much more loopy drunk than high."

I didn't have to ask her to come into my apartment building, and she joined me inside and followed me up the stairs and down a hall.

"This is it," I opened the door of No. 303 and led her into my room.

The first thing she said was, "No wonder you're so depressed."

"What makes you think I'm depressed?"

"You never talk much except tonight, and that's because

85

you're high."

"You don't talk much yourself."

"Yeah," Bridgette walked into the middle of the room, "But I am depressed." She took off her coat and tossed it onto the bed, "There's nothing in this room but furniture, you must be bored all the time." Then, after she swept the room again with her eyes, she said, "You don't have a TV."

"Damn right," I said.

Bridgette sat on my bed.

I said, "I'll admit, this room could use a little decorating, but I'm still getting settled, give me some time."

I thought this whole scene was funny, and began laughing. Bridgette stared at me as I stood in the middle of the room. She sat upright on the bed, her knees together, and her leather jacket lay beside her. The white skin of her neck and arms was an abrupt contrast with her black tank top and pants.

"Bridgette, why aren't you laughing?"

"I'm depressed."

"Foooey," I sat next to her, "What's so depressing?"

"There's no point in living."

"That's dumb," I said, and began laughing again. "What's so funny?"

I was almost in tears, "What's funny is you're right. There is no reason to live. None! I've spent my life worrying about trying to find a reason to live, when I could've tried to enjoy myself. Hearing it from you is so funny."

I assumed what was bothering her was what had bothered me.

"Oh," she sat near me.

I put my arm around her waist. "Bridgette," I kissed her cheek, "Don't be depressed. Okay?"

Her eyes rolled slightly to the ceiling.

"Would you be depressed if I told you I like you?"

She sighed and crossed her arms, "If a silly compliment can make me feel better then I really don't have anything wrong with me."

"What's wrong with you, then?"

"I don't know."

"Oh yeah?" I started tickling her, she smiled, and I kept

tickling her. She fell back on the bed, her arms still crossed over her rib cage, twisting and turning.

"Stop it!" but she was giggling, and I pulled her to me and kissed her on the lips. After a few kisses more she whispered in my ear, "Do you really like me?"

"I really do."

And we kissed for a while.

I was prepared to lose my virginity. I halted for a moment to take off my shoes and socks, and turn off the lights.

I returned, "I'm glad I found you, Bridgette. I think we both have a black cloud inside. Maybe we can make each other happier."

"What's wrong with you?"

"I've just fucked up my life. Then my father died this summer. But, I suppose things could be worse. Just look at all the bums."

I took off her tank top and fumbled around with her bra until she helped me take it off. Her breasts were small and soft. Delicately, I kissed her nipples and curves, feeling ribs underneath her skin. Soon we were in our underpants, and I told her, "I'd like to make love to you, I really would, and you'll probably find this difficult to believe, but I'm a virgin." I held her jawbone in my hand as gently as I would a hollow eggshell "So I don't know how."

My hand slid from underneath her jaw to her shoulder blade and then around her back. We were facing one another.

She said, slowly blinking and wide-eyed, "I'd like to have sex with you, but not now, not tonight. I've been hurt before, and I don't want to be hurt. I'm scared. And I don't want to feel cold ever again."

So my desire was forced to patience, and we slept. From the bed I could only see the night, and this is what I remember; the shadows and shades of gray and black forming prisms on the wall, an engine revving in the distance, and Bridgette clinging to me; and I wondered.

Morning came and I awoke before Bridgette, but I waited until she opened her eyes. She stood up then walked to the bathroom, shivering in the stark air. She was beautiful.

Bridgette returned to the warmth of the bed, and we embraced. Almost without moving my lips I placed them on the top of her nose, her chin, her cheek, her ears, her lips, and her brow. I started kissing her body, from the neck down her shoulder, and all the way up an arm. When I reached her wrist I noticed a thin pink scar. It was straight and began just beneath the palm and went in at almost a forty-five degree angle for two inches. It was about a millimeter wide and was indented convexly in the skin.

I stopped kissing her, and put my arms around her. It seemed like we stayed like that for a half hour, without speaking. This scar was a twinge. Had she tried to kill herself or was it the result of an accident? I went over the type of sharp instrument that might have inflicted the wound.

Perhaps she had been mugged at knife point. But all I had to do was ask.

Instead, we dressed and exchanged short remarks. I walked her home. At her door we said goodbye. I told her I'd had a very nice time, and I'd call her soon. That evening, when I called, however, she wasn't home. So I spent my time reading for school. Later, after midnight, I contemplated the discussion the previous night. And evil. I wrote:

There are some forms of evil that are undeniably wrong and immoral, and thus can be considered evil; rape, murder, torture, and on a lesser degree, deceit, petty thievery, and so on. But there is a lot of middle ground between good and evil. Pleasure has been considered both good and evil. But when ignorance is the root of evil, when people are self-righteous and only understand their own perceptions, when leaders cite glory or whatever reason they use as justification for war, when religion condemns people to hell and men are judgmental, then evil becomes more complex and the cause is ignorant to the effect. The result is hate and hypocrisy. Things such as religion, sex, or drugs, cause evil; but are not evil in themselves, it takes ignorance to turn pleasures and creeds into evil.

I wonder where I fit in all this. I'm learning that to base my opinions on a set of values is not right, except for myself, yet I want to have a set of values, and I want to believe they should apply to everyone. And yet I'm asking myself more and more the questions; Why should I bother? Is life futile? Is my fear increasing? I wonder if I should try and please myself....

I was troubled by the apparent conflict between pleasure and morality, unaware there need not be any battle between the two, for in both pleasure and morality there is good and evil.

The next time I saw Bridgette was in class on Monday. That afternoon we met and ate lunch at a Chinese restaurant. Over the meal I said to her, "So, tell me about yourself."

She told me where she had gone to school.

"Okay, you went to school. Is that it?"

"Yeah, I had a pretty normal childhood."

"Didn't you have any friends?"

"Yeah , sort of. "

"Where are they?"

"Nathan's a friend."

I figured I'd talk about myself since I didn't want to sit in silence, "Well, I had no friends at all in high school except this girl who I went out with, and that was during my senior year." I paused, "I'll always wonder whether I missed something by being a loner. I guess I can't complain, my life's been fairly easy. Any misery I've had has been from mental anguish. Hmmm, I guess all misery, even the physical, is actually mental, because when one is hungry one feels mental pain even though the hunger is physical."

Bridgette didn't say anything.

I continued, "But I suppose everyone needs to suffer so they can appreciate the good things in life."

Bridgette surprised me by exclaiming, "That's bullshit!"

"What?"

"That's no excuse. We don't need misery to appreciate good. I could do just fine without pain the rest of my life."

"Yeah," I nodded my head, "That makes sense."

Bridgette kept looking at me. I found it difficult to sustain a monologue. Every question I asked her she answered as shortly and concisely as she could. I made exasperating comparisons. I had enjoyed conversing with Julie, with Bridgette every word seemed unnatural, perpetually I was asking myself what I should say. And when we were silent she looked at me with that stare, and I couldn't tell if she was questioning me, if she was complacent or if inside her she was continually uneasy. After eating we walked to her house. I told her I'd see her in class, kissed her on the cheek and left.

Bridgette didn't attend class on Tuesday or Wednesday. I spent my time writing a paper that was due on Thursday. Thursday she showed up at the end of class and handed in her paper. In the hall I asked her where she'd been.

She said, "I just haven't felt like going to class."

Part of me wanted to shake her. I was exasperated, but I said, "Well, I miss you. Do you want to go out again this Friday?"

She nodded.

"I got a dial tone this morning. Here's my phone number."

She wrote it down and looked up with a slight smile, which I returned.

I squeezed her hand, "Bridgette, believe me, I like you. Cheer up, please?"

She almost grinned, and I kissed her on the lips right there in the hallway. Her nose-ring had ceased to bother me. I said, "I'll see you in class tomorrow, then."

Friday she came to class, and seemed in good spirits. After class she came over to my desk as I was gathering my books into my tote bag. We were the last to walk out of the classroom, and held hands as we did. She didn't say anything, but it was nice to see her face with a smile. It wasn't like with Julie, where I was simply excited, and then infatuated with the idea of romance, and subsequently hit it off with her. It wasn't that I was falling in love. It was that I felt needed, that I mattered to someone.

We separated in the hallway, and went to our next classes.

That afternoon in my room I contemplated; choosing not to write, for my thoughts were becoming too similar, too monotonous, centering around things that I may never have or know.

I called my mother but there was no answer.

In the evening Bridgette and I met on Broadway and went to Nathan's. We arrived to find Perry and Nathan inside. I sat by Perry on the couch as Nathan and Bridgette conversed.

Perry was twenty-two years old and a fifth-year senior at Seattle University. He would graduate with an English degree in the spring. All his life he'd lived in Seattle, and had gone to a school in North Seattle, which was where he'd met Nathan. Nathan currently didn't work or go to school. Perry told me that Bridgette had gone out with an old acquaintance of Nathan's, and that was why she and Nathan were good friends.

I asked him what college had done for him, and he replied, "The most important thing I've learned is the benefits of education; how to learn and the extent of knowledge that exists. If there is anything I wish to do, learn, or think about, then I can weigh the advantages and disadvantages and make a sound choice. As for my English degree, I like to read. Financially I doubt it will be of any benefit, unless I go to grad school or decide to teach. Grad school's out, for now, I've had it with the intellectual masturbaters at college, they stress too much importance on education and whether or not someone has a graduate degree. In college, life seems alive because you can think about it vividly, big deal; outside college it is alive because you are living it. I've thought about teaching later on, and actually it has its appealing aspects, but the cons outweigh the pros; besides, I'd have to cut my hair, although some schools I'm sure are liberal about that sort of stuff. It's funny, I don't fit in at all at college. It's a Catholic school, and even though the students are fairly normal in that they drink and party, I kinda stick out. But my parents wanted me to go there, so I did."

"What are you gonna do after school?"

Perry scratched his head, "Beats me."

"What do you like to read?"

"I like Henry Miller. That guy knows everything there is to know about life."

"Henry Miller, huh? Tell me where I could find him?"

"Most any bookstore should have him. Start off with *The Tropics*. You'll get into them."

"Great, I will."

Nathan came in, and soon the bong was passed around. We smoked and listened to music and Bridgette and I sat together on the end of the couch. I went through my spell of coughing and eventually was saturated with the high. Bridgette practically sat on my lap and Perry sat at the opposite end of the couch. I enjoyed thinking when high, for life seemed easy.

Perry asked me, "So, what's your story, where're you from?"

I told him about my town, and I told him about how I aimed on talking to God, "I would think shit like, I acknowledge that I have a propensity for desiring the finer things in life like the appreciation of life accumulated through wisdom. If I could only talk to God. No shit. That's written in my journal. And I was completely sober. I got high the first time in my life here last Friday, and I've only been drunk once, so I don't know how I got so fucked up."

Perry and Nathan were smiling, and I could tell they were listening, as well as Bridgette.

"No shit!" I repeated.

Perry asked, "Man, what was your trip?"

"My trip, and this I took seriously, was to talk to God. No kidding. I waited a whole year after I graduated from high school to literally talk to God. Like I'd be able to sit on his knee and ask, 'Hey God, tell me what's going on. All right?' No joke. I began to believe I'd really get to talk to Him." I was enjoying myself, "What's more, and listen to this, I tried to faith heal someone. No shit. I went camping with my girlfriend at the time, and she cut her leg real bad and here comes me, the anti-Paul, with my magic hands. Did I ever feel like a geek. Man, it's funny now, it's real funny."

"Yeah it is." Perry, lit the bong, passed it to Nathan, and reiterated, "It's too weird."

"Yup," I stopped laughing.

I was given the bong. My thoughts drifted to Bridgette, but she was just sitting there so I drifted to the demon book; what a silly fucking book, with it's warning of demons. It is very easy to see effects of humanity's actions and invent a cause. Every thought ended with a reflective 'maybe', and then a different thought replaced it.

We were at a peak high. Bridgette hardly said a word all night. It was after midnight, and I asked her if she wished to leave. She did, and we bade our host goodbye. I thanked Nathan for his hospitality, and shook his and Perry's hands. I enjoyed Perry's company, Nathan had said little, and so I had no strong impression of him.

As soon as Bridgette and I were in the alley I put my arm around her and gave her a long kiss. We held hands as we walked to my place.

I asked, "Did you have a good time?"

"Yes."

In my studio she went to the bathroom. When she came out she took off her jacket, placed it on the table, and glided over to my queen-sized bed. I turned off the light and soon we were making out.

At that moment I was feeling very good, and so I said, "I don't know why, Bridgette, but you make me happy."

Of course, she didn't respond in any manner at all.

So I said, "Your presence, knowing you're close to me, like on Nathan's couch, makes me feel good. My life is improved because you're in it, I think."

She moved slightly in my arms.

And she twitched and stared at me. In the dark I could still see the blue-green of her eyes.

"You're beautiful," I said.

She smiled, and it was a happy smile. Then she giggled, "You're strange."

"And you're beautiful."

We started undressing each other. Completely naked, she helped me inside her. Softly she said, "You can come inside me."

"Won't you get pregnant?" For a second I saw sorrow in her eyes, but the second ended and we continued. She was on top of me, and for the first time I felt what it was like to have my penis inside a vagina. As she started moving her vagina up and down I couldn't believe how good it felt, and I came in a matter of minutes. The whole time the thought 'Shit! This feels good!' was present in my head, for a short moment nothing else existed. Afterwards I began noticing my surroundings, Bridgette's fingers sank into my skin as she pulled me to her; my weight covering her body. This discovery of sex stunned me. I had never masturbated, and, in a sense, I was overwhelmed. Before I knew it I was erect again and we had sex, the second time lasting longer than the first, and ending much better. Sleep was a suitable finish.

In the morning we made love one more time. I couldn't

believe it, sex was so good. No wonder Dennis gave me the free fifth. We dressed, and I gave her a ride home in my Pinto, as it was raining. I hadn't told her I owned a car, and she was glad to have a ride. I told her I'd give her a call.

I called my mother that day.

She answered, and I said, "Hi, it's Paul."

"Oh! How's it going?"

"Okay," I gave her my phone number and a rundown on my life in the city, and school.

She told me how she was doing, "I'm active in church. I'm still meeting the ladies every Wednesday and I even help out part-time at the church's day-care center, it's something I may get to do full-time. How different this house seems with no one in it."

"Are you lonely?"

"Of course, but I'm doing okay. Your father gave me his best, I have no regrets, now I can only look forward to seeing him in heaven."

She told me she was very happy to hear from me and that she loved me. I couldn't get over the feeling of complacency in her voice, as if she had absolutely no concerns, and no pain. I told her I loved her and that I would call in the future.

After we hung up I thought about how nice it would be, when someone dies, to be able to shrug it off and look forward to a reunion in the afterlife. Yes, she sounded composed and able to accept her lot. If she wished to believe in religion, then fine. Religion, to her, was a good thing in life. To me, it was rancid and sour, a lesion. I wasn't sure whether or not God actually existed, but I felt it ludicrous that men thought they could explain Him or it and thus created religion. My mother was a good person, and she believed in religion, but in no ways was she any better a person because she had faith, although she was probably happier. Religion satisfies a need, not a truth.

I began to see Bridgette frequently. In the afternoon we usually met and ate lunch together, and we slept together often, at my place or hers. Her apartment was a small studio, about twenty by twenty, it was cozy and cluttered, with a bed, blankets, a sofa, and pillows that filled the floor, as well a large stuffed kangaroo she had gotten from Nathan when she was in the hospital. I asked her why she had been in the hospital and she said, simply, because she had something wrong with her. I didn't ask more.

There were plants, a television set, a desk, and a bookcase. On the wall was a print by Monet. I looked over the titles in the bookcase, there was some fantasy and horror mixed in with textbooks. I noticed *The Bell Jar*, by Sylvia Plath. Bridgette was a year younger than me, and supported herself by financial aid.

She gave me a plant for my room, as well as some candles and incense. I never pried much into her life, or, at least, I never demanded answers to my questions, nor did I ask her about the scar or her past.

One afternoon I found a bookstore, and I went in and asked the balding clerk where I could find *The Tropics,* by Henry Miller. He looked through his glasses and drolly said, "In the literature section, try 'M.'"

The literature section was directly behind me, and I found *Tropic of Cancer.* I began reading that evening. The first thing that struck me was his ego. He had a firm belief in himself, and little shame in saying what was on his mind. I liked the way Miller was well read, and that he worshipped art, life, and literature. I thought of a quote by Whitman, "...this is no book. Who touches this, touches a man." However, Miller spoke of women in a way I didn't like, "When I looked down into this fucked-out cunt of a whore I feel the world beneath me..." but maybe it was good that I was shocked. It made me think. What was intercourse without love? What is fucking? Maybe his reference to the act of love was offensive, but, even so, it was interesting. Truly Miller didn't know everything there is know about life, but he was full of life, and it was very strange to know that now he was dead. And what had he come to? His writing would continue to cause people to think long after he died; people like me, people who admire anyone who bled his soul to write.

And I thought of *The Bible.* Now there was a book I didn't understand. Once I felt my knowledge of it was sufficient. Ha. I could read *The Bible* every living waking moment of my life, well into the twenty-first century and never grasp its meaning.

Between schoolwork and Bridgette I had little time for anything else. Bridgette and I went to Nathan's and got high every now and then. We never drank or smoked anything when we were alone. I was thankful Bridgette didn't smoke cigarettes. Smoking, there was something I couldn't understand. Perry and Nathan smoked cigarettes, everywhere I turned it seemed like someone was lighting up or putting one out. I just couldn't understand it.

My room began to feel cozy with Bridgette's plant, candles, and presence. I even had a clock radio which could get a few local stations with clarity, so we could listen to music. I enjoyed those intimate nights; soft light flickering, jasmine, cinnamon and hyacinth scents, music with infrequent interruptions by late-night DJ's; I enjoyed those nights.

Once I said to Bridgette, as we were naked in bed, hours after smoking pot, and in a creamy state resulting from just having sex, "You know, Bridgette, I like pot, but sometimes I wonder about it. When I'm high and with you things seem okay, it seems strange to go to school and worry about life when all I could do is be high and make love to you. But sometimes I feel I'm missing something, that it can't last, and that I'll wake up when I'm thirty years old with nothing but my youth diminished. I'm not sure pot is good or not, what do you think?"

"I don't."

"Yeah you do."

She rolled on top of me and folded her arms on my chest. Looking down at me she said, "I don't care when I'm thirty."

I looked at her but her eyes had closed.

So I kept talking, "I wonder if I'm wasting my time by getting high. Sure, at times it seems like I'm opening my mind, and in a way it is, but at the same time I find myself apathetic. About my past and future, everything. I haven't written anything in two weeks."

"Oh," she nudged up against me and we fell asleep.

The next day, after she'd gone, I convinced myself to write, more because I hadn't written much recently than any com-pulsion to think. I tried to write something about sex and Bridgette and indifference, yet was uninspired. Bridgette gave me no emotional bond, and I didn't know why, and I wasn't concerned enough about it to care much. Bridgette never opened up. I can't remember any extended speech of hers. Occasionally I could make her giggle, but her solemn expression would return as soon as the moment was over. When we had sex she barely would make a sound, except a murmur, and a gentle gasp at climax.

November came. I had talked with my mother at regular intervals, and she still seemed calm. I did my schoolwork diligently and with little enthusiasm.

In a month I had gotten to know Nathan and Perry, as well as a couple other regulars, Sonya and Trish. I was comfortable with this group. Yet those evenings at Nathan's were becoming predictable, and my enjoyment of them lessened, but I kept going there with Bridgette. Pot was making me almost complacent. Sitting on the couch, with Bridgette nearby, I would observe. Nathan talked as little as Bridgette, and was always high. Perry impressed me as one who took pleasure in life and wasn't bothered by much, as if this joke of a world was fucked up because it deserved to be, but it wasn't his business. Perry was the only person there whom I had spoken with much.

In the middle of November I went to Nathan's by myself, as Bridgette wasn't feeling well. I was bored and felt like getting high that night. Bridgette said it'd be all right if I went. Perry, Sonya, and Trish were there. Nathan asked me where Bridgette was.

"She's sick."

"Bad?"

"No, she'll come through."

"Good. She's a sweet girl, I hope you treat her good," he gave me a beer and stayed in the kitchen with his bottle. I suspected Nathan sold drugs. Every so often there would be a knock on his door, and Nathan would go to the kitchen and attend to his guest's needs.

At any rate, I sat next to Perry on the couch and proceeded to get high.

Perry said, "So, what made you decide to come by yourself?"

"The pleasure of your company."

"Bullshit, you came over to smoke some doobage."

"I wouldn't do anything like that."

Perry smiled and pulled out his baggie. Using Nathan's bong we smoked the pot.

"You know," Perry mused, "Webster defines marijuana as, 'a narcotic from the hemp plant's dried leaves and flowers, smoked in cigarettes by addicts.'"

"No shit."

"Yeah, if you smoke pot, then, by definition, you're an addict. That's so nearsighted it's Christian."

I became rather baked, and my thoughts wandered, I asked Perry, "You ever give bums money?"

"Rarely."

"I never have, I can't trust 'em."

Perry said, "I know what you mean. Some use the streets as a cover to sell drugs. Others are just fucks, they're too lazy to work. Some really need help. This guy I knew once threw a punch at a bum with a sign around his neck saying 'I'm Blind.' The man flinched."

The plan for the evening was we would attend a small get-together a couple blocks away. So we left, derelicts, four in leather, one in an army jacket. Sonya's head was shaved on one side, above her ear. Both her ears had lots of earrings and studs, and the cropped hair she did have was medium length. In her black leather she was thin, not slender but bony. Trish was shorter than Sonya, with long hair dyed jet black. She had a large bust, wore a lot of makeup, and while she wasn't stunningly beautiful she was sexy and voluptuous.

I was walking next to Nathan, and I asked him, "How do you know Bridgette?" Bridgette hadn't told me anything about her and Nathan except that they were good friends.

"She went out with an ex-friend of mine."

"An ex-friend?"

"Yeah," Nathan shook his head, "He was an asshole to her. They went out for a year and he left her devastated. I became her friend, she needs someone."

"What do you mean?"

"Well-," he hesitated.

98

"Tell me, I can't get anything from her. I ask her things and she doesn't say a peep."

Nathan nodded slowly, "Okay, after she and Ronnie had gone out for a time she got pregnant. Ronnie didn't want anything to do with her unless she got an abortion. She wanted to have the kid but she didn't want to lose Ronnie. So she had the abortion. Ronnie was into heavy drugs and couldn't handle the situation and he broke up. That was a year ago, you're the first guy she's seen since."

Nathan lit a cigarette and went on, "Bridgette was fucked up anyway. Her father left her mother before she was old enough to remember him. Her mother remarried when she was twelve, but that marriage lasted less than a year. She's never had a family or friends. She's pretty, and quiet, so all the girls at school probably thought she was stuck up. So I'm her friend, and I love her as a friend. She needs someone. I know she's got a lot of trips, but she's a good girl."

"I hear you," I nodded as Perry, Sonya, and Trish walked ahead, "That explains some things. It doesn't explain other things. Hmmm."

This information about Bridgette affected me in more ways than one. I felt sympathy for her hardships. I still wanted to know about the scar, but I didn't want to ask Nathan about it. Bridgette always seemed disconsolate, thus I would feel helpless. Yet she was too taciturn. That I heard all of this from Nathan was somewhat annoying. I didn't wish to be a counselor. I thought, if she would ask me for help, if she could tell me of her struggles, I would be willing to try and understand them. But if she wasn't going to help herself how could I help her? Part of me wanted to get close to her, and another part desired to terminate the relationship.

For all the times we fucked and enjoyed it I felt empty, I didn't want to hurt her, which I might do if she was strongly attached to me, yet I wasn't thrilled that she could have sex with me and not make an attempt to be emotionally intimate. My leaving her might increase her pain, and I didn't want to be responsible for that, but I was bothered that she couldn't take care of herself. I never considered the truth - that I was insensitive.

We arrived at a basement apartment underneath a brick building, and we walked down four steps to reach the door. The living room was immediately behind the door, and, in the back of the room was a kitchen on the right and a hall on the left leading to more rooms. The living room was large, with two couches, a coffee table, a couple chairs, and a table. A stereo was against the wall next to a bookcase. The light emitted from the two lamps in opposite corners of the room was red, making every object in the room appear scarlet, burnt orange, blood red, or maroon; black objects appeared purplish and white ones yellow-orange. Against the wall were amps and a keyboard. Guitar cases, in which I assumed had guitars inside, sat next to the amps. In the center of the table was a wooden bowl that served as a stand for a great big candle which was surrounded by smaller candles, all lit. Guitar magazines were stacked by the couch.

Perry came up to me and said he was going on a beer run. I gave him a couple dollars for his collection and he left. Nathan introduced me to the residents, Mike and Sheffield. I was having a difficult time trying to define the word weird, for everyone there had unusual clothing and hairstyles, and they all wore earrings. I stood out the most in terms of dress. Perry returned from the store with a case of beer.

My hair had gotten longer, it almost went over my ears and had reached my shoulders, but aside from that I still wore jeans, my army jacket, and high-top tennis shoes. Sheffield wore a nose ring and had four earrings in his right ear and a two-inch cross dangling from his left. In front his hair stood straight a good five inches on top his head, yet behind it went down about to the center of his back. What was the point in this attire? I thought all this vanity missed a point, or maybe the point didn't exist.

They were watching television, and a McDonald's commercial came on. Sheffield complained, "McDonald's is bullshit. They're killing the rain forests with their Styrofoam shit."

"Yeah, so what're you gonna do about it?" Perry asked.

"Not eat there."

Perry put his hands behind his head, "Do you vote?"

"No, but I ain't got a thing to say about politics, man."

"I doubt that," Perry said.

"I don't, man," Sheffield stuck his right fist into his left hand. "Okay, but politics affect both domestic and foreign problems. The government can have a say in things such as environment, so, when you complain about McDonald's you're complaining about the government."

Sheffield leaned back on the couch, "Fuck that. I ain't gonna eat there because the food tastes like garbage. Heinous, man!"

Perry laughed and turned towards me, "Sheffield's an intense dude."

The television was off, and Mike was trying to find a suitable album. He played a song by The Dehumanizers called 'Kill Lou Guzzo.' Lou Guzzo was a local newsman who was anti-rock and youth, according to Sheffield. It was mayhem, loud and agressive, with crunched vocals; I thought it effective and humorous. We began smoking pot, and I had enough beers to give me a buzz. I stopped drinking, for there was a point with alcohol where I had no desire to go further, besides, the beer began to taste like carbonated urine.

Later that evening the conversation drifted to Vitamin A. I wasn't sure what everyone was talking about. Nathan mentioned he had purchased a sheet of quality blue-dot, and he would have it the following night.

Perry hit me on the shoulder, "You ever take acid?"

"Nope.

"I'm not surprised. Anyway, would you like to try some tomorrow night?"

"Maybe, what the hell is it?"

Perry frowned, and then grinned, "It's LSD, man. Hallucinogenics. I can tell you need to trip."

I went to the bathroom. Now LSD I'd heard of. When I returned my seat had been taken, so I sat between Perry and Trish.

Trish was talking to Perry, and in my stupor I paid no attention to their conversation. But I could smell Trish's perfume, and with her sitting in close proximity I was well aware of her. I leaned sideways on the couch, and was facing her. She was looking at Sonya, and said, "She's so in love with Sheffield."

"Oh, I couldn't tell."

"She's been sitting in his lap all night. She's the only person who'll listen to him as he talks about his music."

"His music?"

"Yeah," she now had turned toward me, and was a foot or so away, "Sheffield's in a band, it's pretty cool, but it's all he talks about. It gets old. She's such a flirt."

I looked at Sonya listening to Sheffield. They were too far away for me to hear what they were saying.

I said, "I guess I can't recognize flirting."

Trish moved closer and tilted her head into my eyes. All that lipstick and eye makeup were distracting. She asked, "So, you can't tell when a girl's flirting?"

"I'm oblivious."

"Uh huh. Well, if I placed my hand on your cheek and played with your hair," she did so, "you wouldn't be able to tell what I was doing?"

"Let's put it this way, if you were flirting with me at this very moment I wouldn't be able to tell one bit."

Trish rolled her eyes, moved a little closer, and put her hand on my knee, "I don't know how to flirt very well, either. It bothers me, because if I wanted to tell you that you turn me on I wouldn't know how to. I'd have to just come out and say it, but as you can see, I'm pretty nervous 'bout stuff like that."

My mouth formed a circle, "Oooh."

We looked hard at each other, "You gonna do acid tomorrow night?"

"Yeah, it's my first time."

"You've never tripped! I'll have to be your guide, then."

"All right," I shrugged.

Perry tapped me on the shoulder, "Hey, I'm going to the store, you wanna come?"

I nodded, said goodbye to Trish, and followed Perry outside. We headed in the direction of the QFC 24-hour grocery store on Broadway. As we walked down the street Perry said, "Listen, what you do is your business, but I noticed you 'n' Trish doin' some heavy pettin'. I know Trish, and I know she's horny, if you know what I mean. Now, correct me if I'm wrong, but you n' Bridgette are goin' out big time; at least you're not afraid to display your affection in front of others. I don't really give a damn what you do, fuck 'em both for all I care, but keep in mind, Nathan cares quite a bit."

"I hear you," I said. Then, "What's the story with Nathan?"

Perry told me, "I went to school with him but I didn't hang with him much. Then I saw him on Capitol Hill a year or so ago and we've hung out ever since. We both like to get high. Nathan's sort of strange, but he's mellow, keeps to himself and his business. You've probably guessed that he deals, he's paranoid about new people hangin' out with him but you were okay 'cause you were with Bridgette. But he's solid, if you know what I mean."

We reached QFC, and started roaming up and down the aisles. We stopped at the candy section.

I asked, "What do you know about Bridgette?"

"Ummm, not much. She's weird, completely difficult to talk to, I don't know how you did it."

"What I want to know is, what about that scar on her wrist? Bridgette evades every question, and I didn't feel right askin' Nathan."

Perry gazed over the candy selection, and I thought he hadn't heard me, but he finally said, "You know about the abortion, don't you?"

I nodded.

"Well, she tried killin' herself right after it. She was a mess. That was about the time I started hangin' out with Nathan. It was intense, I suppose, but I didn't find out about it 'til later. You think she's timid now? That's nothing, she's improved a lot since then."

Perry went to the checkout line with a soda pop and a couple candy bars. He bought me one. Outside he asked me what I wanted to do.

I told him I didn't care, and he suggested we go to his dorm, a few blocks away. On the way he told me about Mike and Sheffield, "They're in this band called Blood Plague, I've heard 'em and they're pretty good, but I wouldn't listen to 'em if I were by myself."

We arrived at his dormitory on the campus at Seattle University. It wasn't what I expected, it was huge, twelve stories tall. He lived on the eighth floor. His room was spacious, with a refrigerator, desk, bed, shelves and drawers, a closet and a window with a great view of the city. He had quite a bit of books and an acoustic guitar leaned against his desk. On a shelf stood a liquor bottle with a candle in it, the bottle was coated with different colors of wax drippings. He sat on the bed, leaning against the wall and dangling his legs.

"Have a seat," he said, as he stuffed pillows between his back and the wall.

I sat down, and said, "Your place is not bad."

"Yup, it's home. Shit, it trips me out. I have longer hair at this place than most of the girls. I feel like an oddball, but I can hang with some dudes and chicks. I've made a couple good friends here. If my parents weren't footin' the bill I don't know where I'd be." He laughed and said,

"I'm a wastoid at night, and a scholar in the day."

"And you don't have a clue about the future?"

"After I graduate," he stretched out his arms, "I'll be clueless."

"C'mon.

"Actually, I might start working for my dad, he's a contractor and there's good money in construction. But I'm not too worried about it now."

He grabbed his guitar and started playing.

"That's nice," I said.

"Yeah it is, it's Zeppelin."

"Zeppelin?"

"Uh huh. 'Going to California.'"

"I've never heard of it."

"Never?"

I shrugged and shook my head.

"Shit. You raised by wolves or something? That song's a classic."

"Yeah, I guess I've missed out on things."

Perry leaned his guitar against the closet and went to the drawer. He pulled out a pipe, baggie, and a lighter, "If they ever caught me with this I'd be expelled, wouldn't that be a bummer?"

We took a few hits, and I asked, "Tell me, why do you smoke pot?"

104

Perry leaned forward and handed his pipe to me to take a hit, "I like to. Plain and simple. It mellows me out. Bush don't know what he's talkin' about; we ought to have a war on the war on drugs, it's a fuckin' waste, I tell ya. It's like, 'Hey, we're high! The whole fuckin' country is high, get off our ass and let us enjoy it!' I mean, there are bullshit drugs, like crack and heroine, but pot is pretty innocuous. It's a crime that it's against the law, it really is. Oh well. Hey! Gimme that pipe'"

I was laughing, and gave the pipe back.

He continued, "Yeah, with all the suffering in this world the law's all worried about people like me havin' a good time. Law's like religion, it's for idiots, but people are idiots so they need to have 'em both. Shit almighty."

"I agree," I said as he lit the pipe, "Religion is for idiots, I'm through with it, but I still wonder about what's going on and God and death."

"I think," he scratched his head, "That when you die, you're dead. That's it. We become mold and dirt, that's what the eternal plan is. We're here on earth for about 25,000 days or so, and then we're not. Make the best of it, I say."

"What about the fucked up world?"

"It'll be fucked up whether you help or not, and more likely than not if you try to help the world you'll fuck it up more and probably piss a lot of people off. Look what Christianity's done, those brainwashed fools. Christianity's okay, it's even good, when its passive; but as soon as they start going out into the world and preaching and trying to save everyone, it becomes evil. Look at the genocides caused by Christianity in medieval Europe, The Inquisition. Shit, I get a headache just thinkin' about it."

"Hmmm," I mused, "Sounds like you've got a beef with Christianity."

"Damn right I do," Perry exclaimed, "I've got a problem with religion in general. I've been force-fed Catholicism for too long, it makes me want to puke. My whole family's fanatic, I mean, I love them and they love me, but they're a bunch of moon-eyed zombies. For the love of life they'll never see that their dogma is the same dogma of Islam or Hindu or any other chicken-worshipping cult. Yeah, I've got a beef with Christianity, I want to be left alone. Just left alone."

"Yeah, in a way I can relate."

Perry leaned back, "Paul you're a strange guy, a little introverted and you're into yourself a little too much, maybe. But you're not a bad guy, you're strange. I can tell you haven't seen much of the world."

I shrugged and looked at Perry, "One more question. Do you think pot is a major influence in your life?"

Perry thought this question funny, and when he was finished laughing said, "Let's see, I guess I'd have to say yes. It's like playing the guitar. I enjoy playing and I'm a different person because of it. I don't think I'm any better or worse, I'm just different. But I'm content livin' the way I do and I don't mess with other people. I don't see what the fuss is," Perry took another hit.

Soon we became tired, and I thanked Perry for having me over, we exchanged phone numbers, and I told him I'd see him the next evening. I went home, and fell asleep after thinking of Trish.

My mother called me the next day and reminded me about Thanksgiving, which was coming up that week. I planned on going home for the long weekend. As evening approached I showered and dressed, feeling lousy. I didn't have a hangover but I felt listless, nevertheless. As it grew dark my stupor lifted somewhat, I called Bridgette. Sniffling, she told me she wasn't feeling any better.

I called Perry and he told me to meet at Nathan's at eight o'clock. I met Perry and Nathan and the three of us went to Mike and Sheffield's. Sonya and Trish were already there, as well as the two members of Blood Plague.

Each of us paid two bucks apiece for a hit of acid, a tiny, white square of paper that had a blue dot. Following directions I stuck the square in my mouth; after fifteen minutes I swallowed it.

Perry told me what to expect, "It'll take about a half hour to forty-five minutes to hit, and when it does you'll wonder whether or not you're high. But by the time you peak you'll know you're high. As to how it feels, I can't describe it. Your eyes dilate. Watch out for mirrors, you'll trip out on yourself. Colors and shapes will look different. The high'll last you a good long time. Have a nice trip."

We were listening to heavy, distorted sound. It was controlled noise.

There we were, in that red environment which was quite conducive to a high. I concentrated on this lava lamp. In it was a glowing mass of giant, translucent, orange and red blobs which oozed about.

Trish walked over and sat next to me on the couch, "Where'd you go last night?"

"I went over to Perry's."

"Oh. You ready to trip tonight?"

"You bet."

She concurrently punched me on the shoulder and winked at me, "Since it's your first time, you'll have to let me explain how you feel."

"If you could do that I'd marry you." Trish looked absolutely luscious. She was wearing a black skirt that went halfway down her thigh, and fish-net stockings. She wore black eye-liner, and deep red lipstick. Her lips had a very alluring pout.

She smiled, "You feelin' anything?"

"Nope.

"Just you wait," she stood up and went down the hall. I watched her hips sway as those thighs slipped away. My attention was turned back to the lava lamp. Perry came over and I said, "You know what? I think I'm feeling something."

"What do you feel?"

"I'm not sure, it's like I'm wired. Electricity is running through me. I see what they mean by being turned on."

I returned to the couch and concentrated on my high as it strengthened. It was juice, it was new life, it invigorated me. Every concept that came to mind I regarded as genius. My life seemed very comic, for it was meager as compared to the big picture; who was I to think it was important? I was an amoeba in a washing machine. This whole God trip was made by men. It was nonsense and a fabrication.

Everyone was now in the room, and I called Sheffield to me, I had never talked to him outside our introduction. As he stood in front of me with his spiked blonde hair and thick, Neanderthal nose-ring, I asked, "I've gotta know, why the nose-ring?"

107

He gawked at me.

"Do you know Bridgette?"

"Yeah."

"Well, she's my girlfriend, and she wears a nose-ring. I asked her about it once but she got defensive. So I dropped it, but I'd really like to know, what would make someone wear one?"

Sheffield dropped to the couch, his hands made fists, "It's image, man, pure image. It's like, fuck the world! Like I don't give a damn what the world thinks. It's my statement."

"Answer me this," I was amused, "If you don't give a damn what the world thinks, then why do you need to make a statement telling the world you don't care?"

He pursed his lips and, with emphasis, continued, "It's more than that. It says something about me and my individuality. It speaks with my music. When I sing I'm mad, and my nose ring says, 'Hey! Listen to this guy sing, he's mad!' So, it's like, part of me!"

His fist was a couple inches in front of his chin. He had expressed his point well enough. I still thought this whole concept of the nose ring was dumb. But then I considered how I wasn't Sheffield; it would be stupid for me to wear a nose-ring, but if Sheffield wished to wear one I should let him do so without the intrusions of my opinions. I should worry more about how I lived and cease taking parts of life too seriously. I laughed out loud and nodded, "That's pretty cool!"

Standing up I went to Perry, "Perry, I'm high!"

"Cool, man."

Perry must have been high, too, for he was grinning. I realized I was literally fucked up, that I thought in a different manner, and this was extraordinarily refreshing. On the wall was a picture of a snake wrapped around a woman, the two were at the base of a tree in a thick, tropical jungle. Birds, flowers, and vines made the picture an intense visual display. It wriggled and squirmed, the edges where the colors changed flittered, and in a way the picture appeared to have more than two dimensions.

Perry came over, and I said, "This-" my hands rolled outward, "This is unexpected. I thought that taking hallucinogenics meant seeing insects or monsters or blood gushing out of the wall.

Look at this!" I pointed at the picture.

Perry glanced at it, "Yup. It's something."

"No shit," and I kept staring at the wall. Perry walked away.

Trish came up behind me, "How's it going, dude?"

Dude? I looked at her, "It's going." I gazed into her hair, "Trish, your hair is so black. Black! Everything else is dancing but your hair, it's so black."

She laughed and hooked her arm around mine, "C-'mon, we're gonna take a walk."

"We?"

"Yeah, Mike knows of a party a few blocks away. Wouldn't it be cool to trip out on other people?"

"Noooh," I put my hand to my forehead.

She poked me in the stomach, "It won't be that bad."

She led me outside, where the rest of our clan had already gathered. I wondered how anyone on acid could organize anything, and I thought it likely we would get lost on the way to the party.

It was a little after nine o'clock. The air was crisp and cold and chilly. There were no clouds but the stars were hidden by the dark haze of lights reflecting on the ceiling of the sky. I could see the half moon, however. We headed toward Broadway, and then walked through the night life.

Instead of taking in surroundings as a whole, I would notice specific things. Like a plant in the window of a store, or a lighted sign a hundred yards in the distance, or the music thundering from a car's stereo as it drove by.

Broadway was a mass of foreign bodies. Faces were blotches; a grotesquerie of humans, with their slurred and painted faces, and all had a look of desperation and futility. Voices sounded as if they were directed at me but they couldn't have been. These nameless faces depressed me; I had never had so much scorn for this feckless human race. We were freaks and it didn't matter. There was no sense in searching for meaning when it wasn't meaningful, and then I was struck with what I considered profound thought: the whole key to existence lay hidden in the ultimate paradox. Bells, buzzers, and lights went off frenetically. This was it! It had come to me, all of a sudden I had found the answer. The key to existence lay hidden in the ultimate paradox. It explained contradiction, the futility of my search. This was the theme for my trip, and I repeated it in my head.

Often I would forget I was with others. I would panic, and then find a familiar face and security. This happened more than once. We finally reached our destination, a place a block off Broadway and near Pine. It wasn't too far from my apartment. The party was on the ground floor of this huge, brown house. There might have been forty or so people in the main room, milling about, holding yellow plastic cups filled with tepid beer, and making a lot of noise. The music was loud, competing with voices to be heard, and I was not at ease, but it was a different discomfort I had felt than at the party I had been to in high school with Dennis. Instead of being in a shell I simply disliked this party scene. What a menagerie.

I turned, "Perry!" He was standing near the entrance, all other members of our group had gone inside. I asked him, "Why are we here?"

"It's the thing to do, man. I'm sure we won't stay here for too long. Let's go in and see what's going on."

I followed him inside, but I soon lost track of him. The music was loud, and it refracted the shouts and yells of the party inaudibly. I found a corner of the room to stand in and watched. There was a mix of people, some had an appearance of normality, in that they had short hair and looked clean-cut, others were on the Trish or Sheffield side of the spectrum. There was nothing to fear, it was only a large party. I thought about my ultimate paradox.

Trish popped out of nowhere, and careened in front of me, "How's it going?"

"Okay, I guess."

"You're pretty high, aren't you?"

I could feel my tongue in my mouth, "If you say so. I kinda want to leave."

She grabbed my hand and led me through the crowded room, in and out of a kitchen, and out a door. We ended up in an alley behind the house.

"It's loud in there."

"This is true," I nodded.

"What're you trippin" on?"

So I told her, "All right, this is it. The key to existence is hidden in the ultimate paradox."

"Huh," she shook her head, "That's too deep for me."

And so I babbled, "No it's not, it's quite simple, listen. There is an answer to all our problems. People want to know 'Why?' We desire to know our purpose, and whether or not there's a God. Well, we can't, we won't, and we will never know. That's the answer. Let me explain the ultimate paradox. The answer is," I couldn't tell about Trish, but I was hanging on my every word, "The answer is - there is no answer! Okay, so what we must do is realize the contradiction exists. If we could just be satisfied in knowing there is no answer, or that if there is an answer we will never discover it, then we would be making a great step towards making the world a better place. There, I'm finished." My, hands were clasped, and I released them as if I were dropping a water balloon at her feet.

She put her hand on her forehead, "Shit, that's too intense. I'm gonna explode. You must be fried out of your mind."

"I think I am."

We were no more than two feet from each other. Underneath her jacket she wore a black shirt that covered one shoulder and went at an angle above her chest so that the top of one of her breasts was exposed. Her other shoulder was bare except for a black bra strap. She wore a black belt around her waist.

I asked her, "Do you want to be here anymore?"

"I don't know," she tilted her head slightly and curled a smile.

"I don't. I live a couple blocks away from here. You want to go there?"

"Yeah, wait, I'll go tell Sonya I'm leaving," she went back in to the party and returned soon afterwards. She locked her elbow in mine. We walked out onto the street and down to Bellevue. As we passed a bum she said, "I feel bad for bums, I really do, I don't see how they can live. I don't know how I'd handle such desperation. I could never get like that, they're not even people, they're just bums."

Instead of responding to her comment, I asked, "Trish? I'm

curious, how many times have you dropped acid?"

"I don't know."

"Would you say over ten times?"

"Yeah."

"How 'bout twenty-five?"

"I don't know."

"Doesn't the thrill ever leave? Doesn't it get old?"

She laughed, "Does sex ever get old?"

I didn't answer.

She said, "I've got my Nine Inch Nails with me."

"What?"

But she only smiled.

I couldn't see myself taking acid much, it was okay to experience once, but it wasn't better than reality, only different. I thought of Bridgette, where was she? The world would keep turning, in a hundred years we'd all be dead, and if people wanted to fornicate what did it matter? Nothing. So if I wanted to please myself I could. Trish represented sex, the ends of my desire, from her black eye-liner and hair, her pouty lips and large bust, to her curved waist and thighs; from the feel of her leather jacket, cold and hard as it brushed against me, her black purse over her shoulder, to the rustle of her clothing. She was snake charmer and I cobra.

The entire walk to my apartment, up stairs and into my room, was filled with anticipation. Inside, Trish exclaimed, "Dude! This is totally mundane. How can you stand living here?" She stood in the center of the room, and I placed myself a foot in front of her, "I can't, that's why I invited you here."

She looked around, "Where's your stereo?"

"I don't have one."

"Shit."

"I'm sorry, I hope you'll live," I put my arms around her and kissed her on the mouth, slipping my tongue through the opening between her lips. My hands felt her back as it squirmed underneath the leather jacket.

In a matter of seconds the lights were off and we were on my bed. I asked, "Aren't you curious about Bridgette and me?"

She bit my ear and laughed, "Who's Bridgette?"

Then, as if there were a chance of forgetting, I forced myself to turn on a lamp and write on a piece of paper, 'The key to existence is hidden in the ultimate paradox.'

"What're you doin'?" Trish asked.

"Sorry 'bout that, had to get it out, now I' m ready."

We started kissing again, and she said, "How do you live without a stereo?"

"I'm not sure."

As the last piece of clothing was kicked off the bed Trish said, "Paul, you don't know how much I want this."

"As much as me, I think?"

I kissed her nakedness as she lay underneath me, the lights and sound were background, the center of my attention was Trish, everything else pirouetted in and out of my conscious. My tongue licked every part of her body, and she moaned as she said, "Paul, look at me."

I did. Her eyes were two different colors of black, impenetrable darkness surrounded by a chasm of emptiness.

She parted her lips, "Fuck me."

I was thinking; every movement revolves around my penis inside this vagina, this vagina belongs to a person but it doesn't really matter who as long as she is attractive. Every movement of sex added to a created reality, a sense of now, of only one reason of being. This ecstasy of sex surpassed anything I had felt with Bridgette. Bridgette made me feel if I wasn't careful she might break down and cry. With Trish, I could do what I wished, both our wills were committed to intensifying the sexual act.

I was wired, and I was surprised at how long I could fuck. It seemed like it would never end. Every stroke and caress produced an oooh or an aaah. When we came it was loud and long.

Yet we couldn't stop, we kept licking and kissing one another, and fucked twice more. The second time was as powerful as the first, but as we were fucking for the third time my perception changed. Suddenly I felt a change, a transformation from confusion to acumen, it was almost objectivity. I had lucid and scattered thoughts; I was on drugs, having sex, for my own pleasure. I hadn't given a damn about Bridgette, and, for that matter, Trish. The sex determined what I did, but my will didn't equal my desire. I had no affection for Trish, and although I felt ambiguously about Bridgette I did care for her. As Trish moaned I began to loathe myself. My penis throbbed with pleasure, and I didn't want the sex to end, for when it did I'd have to face the rest of my life. When orgasm came I practically screamed, for seconds all was justified, then it was over. As Trish cooed in my ear and nestled against me I stared at the ceiling. She breathed rhythmically in her sleep as I struggled to remain motionless.

In the calm of before morning she looked attractive in her placid state, naked with a sheet half covering her from the waist below, yet the lust had gone. I lay beside her, not touching her, staring at her and waiting for dawn, wondering how what had for a moment stopped all sense of time could slip irrevocably into the past.

I could not sleep, and as the sky brightened I swung my legs over the side of the bed, stepped over the scattered clothing, and went to the bathroom. I took a shower, dressed, and fixed myself a bowl of cereal and milk.

My apartment was depressing, or maybe it was me. On the window sill was a jade plant Bridgette had given me. It was small, with its rubbery leaves reflecting light. It made me sad to look at it. I found my piece of paper, with my ultimate paradox, and I crumpled it into a tiny ball and flicked it in the direction of the trash basket. I sat in a chair across from my bed and singularly noticed each moment pass.

Trish awoke, and got dressed in front of me. She asked, "How long've you been up?"

"A while."

She went to the bathroom and washed up. When she came out she wore no makeup. As she put on her earrings she looked at me, "Why are you so quiet?"

I hadn't moved from my seat, and let out a breath, "I feel bad. About last night," I paused, then, "I care about Bridgette. It's not your fault."

Without emotion, she asked, "You want me to leave?"

I didn't say anything.

"Don't worry, I'll leave." She walked to and opened the door.

"Trish?"

In the doorway she turned and stared back at me.

"Trish, please, I don't want Bridgette to be hurt."

With her eyes that had been so black, she looked at me, "When you have a one night stand you should expect what comes with the territory."

And the door closed.

That day my thoughts were swirling, I wrote down on paper what I could of what was in my scattered mind:

> Last night I saw Satan grab his crotch with all the world's evil dwelling in the folds of his testicles, and the terror, rot, and hate creeped into my self. Sex feels so good, but never have I felt so awful, lonely, and empty.
>
> "It seems as if I'm fucked up, and so is everyone else. We're all screwed up and clueless. No one cares about anyone else. What does Trish care about? Life, love, or anything? I never imagined life could be like this. I see nothing. Everywhere I go there is a void. Yet I still think something may be out there. I must be desperately overlooking what it is. Love, maybe. I want to love but right now I can't. I don't even love myself. All I can do is hate. I hate evil and it is in myself and the human race and so I hate everyone...

That afternoon I called Bridgette and asked if I could come over. I found a flower shop on Broadway and bought a pink carnation. Then I went to her little apartment and knocked on the door. She wore sweats and no makeup. Her nose was without its ring, even. I gave her the flower and hugged her.

She invited me inside and I sat on the couch.

I said, "It's good to see you." But it wasn't. It was torture. What was I thinking, that I would feel better because of a flower?

I stayed for about an hour. My strain went unnoticed, I believe, and although we didn't talk much, Bridgette had the television on, I felt she had been cheered by my visit.

On return to my apartment I went to the basement. I wanted to drive, to get away from Capitol Hill. I wound through downtown, past the Space Needle, and drove onto Queen Anne Hill. I found a spot overlooking Puget Sound, with boats, ferries, and buoys in the water. I longed for the Pacific and the swish of trees above my head.

I closed my eyes. In one year so much had changed. My asceticisms and hedonisms had missed the point. I had learned a lot, supposedly, but what had I learned? That I missed the point? That there was no point?

115

I realized my foremost desire in life was to be able to feel good about myself. I wanted a sense of self-worth, to be narcissistic without being selfish, to have confidence in myself so I could give myself to someone. I had always thought my purpose in life should be everyone's and vice-versa, but this wasn't so. There were some things that were right for everyone, and some that were only right for me. I would have to begin to see the many sides and viewpoints of things and consider them all with the realization I wouldn't discover truth. Yet in the back of my mind I wished to be devoid of all this. If I could be content without having to justify.

Bridgette. She was pretty. Her difficulty in expressing herself had no malice. Yet I didn't enjoy her company, I couldn't see myself with her for much longer. The only possibilities for a relationship are termination or marriage. There was no chance of marriage. Of course, I could float with sex and hope for an easy way out, but that didn't appeal to me. Since I couldn't accept a relationship with her, I felt the best thing to do was to remove myself.

I called Bridgette a couple times, and on Tuesday she attended class. She came over as I had planned to leave for the coast after school on Wednesday.

We were in my room, listening to the radio, speaking little. I was as quiet as she was, and she asked, "Why're you so silent?"

I shrugged and glanced at her. She looked at me, eyebrows bent. I finally said, "Bridgette, what do you think about me?"

Her head drew back slightly, and, almost question-like, she answered, "I like you."

"But why?"

"Why what?"

"Why do you like me?"

For some reason I had to know, and she only said, "I don't know."

"Do you like me for my sense of humor?"

She didn't answer.

"My looks?"

I stood up, "I don't even like me. What is there?"

I thought, is it because we fuck? Because we have meaningless sex you feel some sort of feigned intimacy? But I didn't ask that. Instead she came over to me, and said, "I like you, I just do."

We held each other, and sadness crept upon us and we gradually made love. I had told myself I would break up with her on that day, and I ended up having sex with her.

On the drive home I tried to reason with myself. Why couldn't I enjoy the fact I was having sex? Dennis, I thought, would be buying his friends party hats and cigars after a sexual encounter, while for me it added to my confusion.

It was strange being home. I had never had such an extended time away, but still the familiarity of everything made me feel I belonged. I walked in on my mother watching television, as if she had watched it her entire life. She gave me a hug, asked me how I was doing, I told her, and she resumed her interest in the show. All was well at home, so I went outside and stood on the bluff underneath the ash-colored sky and let the drizzle soak my army jacket. This was more like it.

Thanksgiving went fine, my mother was almost cheerful, and if I was in a poor mood it didn't show. I visited my old haunts, the dock, the coast, I even saw the eagle once. On Sunday mother asked me if I wanted to go to church with her. I appreciated the fact that, after I had declined, she did not try to convince me.

As I drove back to Seattle, I remembered when romance had thrilled me, as it had with Julie, and how I thought I could have held her forever. No, it had to have been more than that. It wasn't just a fleeting glimpse into an enigma. Love had to be a reality.

I saw Bridgette in class Monday, and she wondered why I hadn't called her. I told her I had come home late, which was true. We went out that afternoon. It was okay being with her, but I avoided sleeping with her, not inviting her to my place, and when I was over at hers I left because of schoolwork, which I did need to do, but still, it was an excuse.

Friday came, it was the beginning of December, and school was almost over. Bridgette wanted to go to Nathan's that Friday, so I went with her.

The gang was all there; Nathan, Perry, Sonya, and Trish. I went to the couch and sat next to Perry. Trish ignored me, Bridgette sat next to me.

"Long time no see," Perry said.

"True, how's it been goin?"

Perry grinned, "It's goin', still. Man, I got approached in the street the other day by this Christian freak screaming repent, salvation or hell, and all that bullshit. The misguided fuck. I said, 'Go from the presence of a foolish man, if thou hearest not in him words of wisdom.' That's a Proverb, you know."

"Hmmm," I mused. The bong was passed to me, and I took a hit. I noticed Trish make a selection at the stereo.

The high crept into me. I felt apathy swallow me, and for the first time I resented it. I remembered the myth, heard that demon chuckle. Was there any help? The only one able to do anything about myself was myself. I thought about pot and how marijuana accentuated desire for pleasure, emotions magnified and diminished. If one sincerely desired love and peace, then marijuana made one want to love and be peaceful. No wonder the Sixties were so controversial. I think they proved that the desire to love and be peaceful is uncommon in humans, in the same way that religion has proven it, for how many of the religious or the drugged-out truly wish good-will upon humanity? They'd rather have judgment and religious wars, or the ultimate high. People didn't care about peace-for-everyone, people only wanted to be happy, and there weren't and aren't many whose happiness depends upon their living a decent life. Their happiness depends on pleasures and securities. Most people didn't care about anyone else except friends and family. Still, the peace movement grew admirably, yet it failed, and it might have been because no matter how much the individual desired to make the world a better place, it came down to the drug and pleasing oneself. Yes, I thought, but what do I know?

The strange sounds we listened to there. The lyrics went through my head, music that matched my state, with words of sin, animosity, and sexual intensity, but what use is there in trying to describe music?

I went to the bathroom. When I came out Trish met me and

118

said, "Nathan asked me what we did that night. I told him we didn't want to hang out at the party so we took a bus downtown and tripped out all night."

I nodded, and she went into the bathroom.

Back in the living room I resumed my seat, next to Bridgette.

Bridgette's presence was beginning to grate on me. Her affection had become baggage. I wanted an individual, a true companion whom I could talk to and share thoughts and lives with; not someone who would listen to me as I expounded on my own ideas.

I never felt animosity as I did that night. It wasn't directed at anyone, it simply was present inside myself. All my life I'd never had an enemy, I never had cause to hate. My greatest adversary had been ennui. But as I sat in Nathan's living room, poison seeped into every part of my self. There is a purity of the soul, a wholeness, an enlightenment one feels when engrossed with the beauty of the world. My current state was the opposite. All pleasure vanished and a darkness emanated. It was universal hate, and it was strong, it didn't seem to come from within yet I could feel it trying to consume me.

And I hated. I hated Bridgette's weaknesses. I hated Trish because I had fucked her; or maybe I hated the impulse. I blamed Nathan for supplying the drugs without concern about what drugs did to people. I accused Perry of being a captive of pot and a fool who didn't give a damn about anything or anyone. I hated the ignorance in myself and everyone else and all the pain it caused. But most of all I hated myself. I hated my hypocrisy for I despised judgment yet I was being judgmental. I was a vehicle of hate. That in my life I had been granted most amenities and comforts, that I had never experienced vast pain, and still had such an overload of hate, was the cause of my greatest agony.

"Paul, is anything wrong?" Bridgette asked.

I barely moved my lips, "I want to leave."

Standing up, I led her out of the room. Nathan was in the kitchen, and I told him we were leaving. We thanked him for his hospitality and left before any questions were asked. I wanted to have sex, it would be solace, my only outlet to vent out my frustration with any possibility of satisfaction, albeit ephemeral.

119

In my apartment I took mine and her clothes off as we stood in the center of the room. I lowered her to the bed, and as she lay there with legs slightly apart and bent I looked down at her. She was very beautiful, and there was a burning thrill at seeing her naked and realizing I could do whatever I wished to her and that she would enjoy it. I was feeling emotion in currents, desolation and exultation at the same time, was this what life was for? This?

I turned off the lights and went down on her, proceeding to cover her entire body with saliva until she was sticky, wet, and moaning. Then I pushed myself inside her and it was energy, a bolt, I could tell by her eyes that she was startled. And there was little difference between her and Trish. She gasped, like a cat, and we fucked. When I came I pulled out and shot on her stomach and spread the semen over her chest with my hands.

As we stuck to one another the instant gratification passed, it was like the high had worn off.

"Oh, Paul," she squeezed me, "Paul. I love you."

Bridgette could have shoved a knife up my ass and caused as much shock. I just waited until the jolt wore off, however, not saying anything. And in resignation we fell asleep.

In the morning I woke to Bridgette kissing my neck, and I had an erection. We had sex again, slowly, and it was good, almost dreamy all the way through climax. Afterwards I was drained.

And the sorrow returned, filling my bone; thin as bamboo. With blue-green eyes, surrounded by haze as a tear formed she said one more time, "I love you, Paul."

She didn't deserve this. What made her say she loved me? Drenched in shame I looked at her black pupils.

"Do you love me?"

The scar.

I answered, "I don't know. Does it matter?"

She was silent. The only sound was her masticating as she tried to build up the courage to respond.

"You don't love me?"

"I don't think so."

I put my arms around her and pressed her to me, "I can't. If I could I would. It's not you, it's me."

120

I heard every word, seconds after I'd said them as they slowly left the room. Bridgette shivered. Nothing was said as we dressed, and I told her I'd walk her home. So we went through the foggy streets and piercing air to her place.

In her tiny room I sat on the couch, silence seemed to overwhelm, with words coming as from the background, far away, "Bridgette?"

"Yes?"

"I know nothing about you. Tell me something about yourself."

"Like what?"

I felt like a creep, but I persisted, "Like, for example, why do you have a scar on your wrist."

She blinked, "I cut it."

I let go, "After an abortion. It was a suicide attempt, right? I would imagine these things are pretty important in your life, and yet you think you're in love with me and can pretend none of the past ever happened. You don't love me, you just want to love me. And I don't love you, nor can I, and you want to know why? It's because I don't know you, I only know a facade, an image, a sheet of steel wrapped around the soul. Who are you? I don't know, but I know I don't love you."

Tears were beginning to fall from her eyes.

"Don't cry," I placed my hand on her shoulder, "It's not you, it's me, I'm all fucked up. My father died this summer, and I'm all fucked up."

Then something snapped in Bridgette, and for once she was uninhibited. She whipped her head towards me and said, "You're fucked up? Your father died? Well, that's too bad, but my stepfather, he fucked me when I was twelve." She glared at me, and then finished, "So get out because the more you stay the more it hurts." She said this without stammering, almost as if it were rehearsed. Then she started weeping, and I did get out; slithering away.

Epilogue

Bridgette wasn't in class on Monday. I called her that night and she answered, recognizing my voice instantly and saying, "I don't want to talk to you."

I heard the static on the phone line, and said, "Bridgette?" I couldn't tell if she was listening, but she hadn't hung up, "Bridgette ... I'm sorry, don't do anything drastic."

"I'm not a baby!' Her voice startled me, and before I could reply the dial tone was humming in my ear.

She didn't attend class all week. I suppose she could have turned in her final paper to the teacher, but that didn't matter. I went home after that week of finals, sullen and cheerless. Back home I wrote in my journal:

> I searched for God and found death. I wanted love but all I encountered was sex. Yet now I am beginning to see I hadn't a chance, for I thought by simply having a desire to know, and to find out, that I would be satisfied.
>
> I must have had some faith, at some time or other, but now it is difficult for me to believe that once I actually had enough devotion to God to expect that I'd be able to talk with Him. I'm not what I once was. What is truth? Is it relative? Who cares?
>
> I think I shall give up ...

My mother spent her time in her usual ways, playing the piano, watching television, and doing philanthropy through the church. It did my spirit good to see her content with life. I wasn't bothered that her strength came from a psychological phenomena.

Christmas break was a rest I needed. My head began to clear up, probably, I thought, as a result of my body being cleansed from all the pot. I wondered about the future, it seemed barren, I would live a certain amount of years, occasionally experiencing pain and pleasure, but for the most part feeling the boredom in between, and then I'd die.

A week into the break Julie called. I was surprised, and somewhat elated to hear from her. So I picked her up and we drove to the dock. It was cold and windy, so, again, we stayed in my car.

She said, "I heard about your dad dying."

I nodded.

"I'm sorry, it must be tough."

"Yeah, it is. But I'll live, hopefully, for better or worse."

"Do you want to talk about it?"

I turned towards her, "It hurt a lot, I've felt a lot of guilt, but it's over, and there's nothing more to say."

"Oh."

But I said more, "My father's death will never be out of my mind, but I'm beginning to see that being miserable because of it is pointless. It's no excuse for me to be unhappy."

We didn't say anything for a while, so I mentioned, "I went to school."

"You did?"

"Yeah, at a community college in Seattle."

"What'd you think of it?"

"It was okay."

Julie sighed, and we didn't speak for another moment, then she said, "Paul, I've wanted to tell you this for a long time. I've felt really bad about what happened a year ago. I deceived you, it was a rotten thing for me to do. I want to apologize."

I smiled a little, "Apology accepted."

"Thanks," she kissed me on the cheek.

I laughed a little.

"What's so funny?"

"You wouldn't believe it. I'm no longer a virgin, I've done some drugs, and, of course, I'm no longer Christian."

Julie let out a breath, "Whoa, your dad's death really did do something to you."

"Yeah, I've learned that maybe I should have more respect for the living than the unknown. That I should love what I can touch. You know, for the first time I'm not too worried about life, I'll let it take care of itself. Sure, I'll always carry my father with me, but maybe I can learn from it instead of just feeling self-pity."

She put a hand on my shoulder, "I'm so sorry."

I looked at her and she at me for a while, without saying anything. I finally asked, "You still have a boyfriend?"

"You really want to know?"

"I want to know, and be honest."

"No, I don't, you can trust me. But, I want you to know, I'm not going to be turned down a third time."

And then we touched lips and slowly began to kiss.

"Believe me, Julie," I said, hugging her, "You won't be."

And so I didn't know what was in store between Julie and me, but we were young and had plenty of time. A true bond of friendship had formed between us, and that was invaluable.

Yet perhaps one of the most important revelations in my life came after I ran into Dennis. It was a Saturday afternoon, and I was leaving a gas station when I noticed him driving in, and we recognized each other and stopped.

I rolled down my window, as did he, and I said, "Hey, how's the partymobile runnin'?"

"Pretty good."

We talked about what we were doing, I told him I was attending school in Seattle. He was in the painting business. Then he asked, "So, you up for drinking anytime? Or are you still clean and sober?"

"I don't know."

"Still the same guy, huh?"

"Not really. Actually, I wouldn't mind shooting the shit with you some time."

He had nothing planned, and so he followed me to my house. We went inside, past my mother, and up to my bedroom. It was depleted of most of its furnishings, a mattress replaced my old bed, but there were still a couple chairs in which to sit.

"Man, this room is empty."

"Yeah, all my stuff's in Seattle."

The sky was light gray, and fog rolled on the horizon. As I looked out I saw the eagle fly above the ocean, it did a circle and exited out of our view.

I noticed Dennis, who was watching, and I smiled, "That's pretty keen, isn't it?"

"It sure is," he said, and then he put on a solemn expression, "So, Paul, I heard about your father dying. It tripped me out, I mean, maybe you don't want to talk about it, but it just freaked me out. I felt bad when I heard."

"I appreciate that," I sat down, "I'm over it, I hope. I'm different because of it, though."

"I bet."

"I mean, you didn't know me too well, but I've changed a lot. I'm not such an anti-social person now, and I could use a friend or two."

"Really?"

"Yeah, tell me, did I miss out in high school?"

Dennis said, "Maybe, if you think you did then you did."

"I'm not sure, but I don't have much, really. Some memories, most of them sour. You had a good time, didn't you?"

"Hell yeah, high school was the best."

"Hmmm, all I got is this," I picked up my journal, which was lying on the bed. I flipped the pages to show him that it was written in.

Dennis said, "Shit, that's a novel."

"Yup, about two years of my life."

Then we talked about the beauty of nature in our home town, and I asked him about his love life, and he told me he'd had a girlfriend for a while but he didn't know how long it was going to last. We exchanged phone numbers, and as he left I told him, "Give me a call some time, and we'll have a beer."

"Yeah," he smiled, "I'll do that." And we shook hands.

So there I was, in my room with my journal. And I considered that, perhaps, the doggerel I've accumulated might amount to something.

Yes, I thought, I have a story to tell. For the first time I considered the worth of my life, and that I had not wasted my life, that in reliving my life I would learn more than in living it. The harm I'd done had been done mainly to myself. I would examine my life and the people in it. I would try to be less judgmental, although I knew this would take effort. Should I have extended myself more? To my father, or Julie, or Bridgette? I felt badly about Bridgette, and I promised myself I would make an effort to be her friend if she would let me. As for God, I knew that I would never know the essence of what Him or it or the spiritual way is, but that the idea of God is a beautiful idea. My anger with life could never be directed towards a creator, only my gratitude. I saw that it is a pity that mankind abuses such a well of hope and virtue, and a shame that pride dictates humanity only have one God or set of beliefs, although mankind offers hundreds to choose from. And I told myself that I should have realized, all along, that *the most important thing in life is love. To have and to give it.* Now I knew, and a wave of ecstasy flowed through me, purer than anything I had known before. It was divine, as when I felt God had first touched me, but it was more. It was an assurance, a hope, and I will never know whether it came from within or from without. That is a mystery I'll never solve. But I had prayed for guidance, and maybe it had actually come. Whatever it was, it was love, and spirituality and freedom. I saw that spirituality did exist, it was just that religion was a barrier between spirituality and the individual. No longer would I be misled by the fantasies of mankind's yearning to answer what cannot be answered. Yes, I would write, and I would love, and I went to my window in hopes of seeing that eagle fly over this ocean.

Author's Note

This is a first printing of my novel, and although it may prove to be unnecessary I would like to take precautions on the possibility this novel is financially successful at a place in time where I am no longer around to enjoy such fruits of my labor.

Any revenue that would have gone to me I wish to go to charity. The conditions are that such charity is: 1) Not affiliated with any religious or political institution or group. 2) Alleviates suffering - thus it feeds, clothes, shelters, and educates the disadvantaged. (As opposed to charities that take sides on issues we will never be able to agree upon - abortion, capital punishment, and so on. Or recreational charities that buy swimming pools for communities or take busloads of children on ski vacations.)

I am not sure how this final document would stand in a court of law, but nevertheless I stipulate that none of the revenue shall go to a lawyer. I will determine the executor.

Money cannot buy happiness or love, but it can aid in the dissipation of misery, which may give more people a chance to stand on their feet and choose whether or not they wish to love. May humanity make such a decision.

—Caleb Powell